A 1960s
Childhood

A 1960s Childhood

From Thunderbirds to Beatlemania

PAUL FEENEY

To mum and dad

Front cover image: Whit Walks Manchester: A group of young lads seen here in their neighbourhood before taking part in the Manchester Whit Walk parade © Trinity Mirror / Mirrorpix / Alamy

This special edition published 2012
First published 2010
Reprinted 2010, 2011

The History Press
The Mill, Brimscombe Port
Stroud, Gloucestershire, GL5 2QG
www.thehistorypress.co.uk

British Library Cataloguing in Publication Data.
A catalogue record for this book is available from the British Library.

ISBN 978 0 7524 7940 8

Typesetting and origination by The History Press
Manufacturing managed by Jellyfish Print Solutions Ltd
Printed in India

CONTENTS

Acknowledgements   7

One	A Decade of Change	9
Two	Home Life	33
Three	Out on the Streets	55
Four	Games, Hobbies and Pastimes	81
Five	Music, Fashion and Cinema	103
Six	Radio	119
Seven	Television	139
Eight	Schooldays and Holidays	173
Nine	Christmas	195
Ten	Memorable 1960s Events	215
Eleven	Whatever Happened To?	225

Acknowledgements

I would like to thank Gwen Lippingwell for allowing me to reproduce the photograph on page 11. All other pictures and illustrations are from the author's collection. Every reasonable care has been taken to avoid any copyright infringements, but should any valid issue arise then I will look to correct it in subsequent editions.

One

A Decade of Change

It's eight o'clock in the morning on the first day of January 1960, and kids all over the country are dipping freshly cut bread soldiers into the soft yellow yolks of lightly boiled eggs. Just like any other morning, the wireless is already on and Jack de Manio is reading the news on the *Today* programme. Thousands of grown-ups are running late for work, having foolishly believed his inaccurate time-checks. Everyone knows that he is prone to giving out the wrong time during his radio show, it is all part of his laid-back presentation style. He is easy to listen to and can be quite amusing, not at all stuffy like the other BBC newsreaders; even young children happily tolerate his breakfast programme. It's hard to believe that Christmas Day was only a week ago. It now seems like a distant memory. Some

children have already gone back to school, and the rest have just three more days of freedom to enjoy before the dreaded Monday arrives when they too will have to return to school for the start of a new term.

You have just finished the last of your bread soldiers and you are now scraping your spoon around the inside of the eggshell to retrieve every last piece of egg white. There is a cup of tea that's been sat on the table in front of you for about fifteen minutes, and it's now cold. You've been day-dreaming and it's taking you absolutely ages to eat your breakfast. Meanwhile, your mum is bustling about the room, trying to clear the table around you, but you are oblivious to her loud tutting, too engrossed in your own thoughts and in no rush to finish.

As amazing as your daydreams may be, your imagination will never stretch to encompass all of the astonishing delights that future years will bring to improve the lifestyle that you so readily accept as normal on this, the first day of 1960. Could it be that one day, ordinary people will have their whole house centrally heated and families will no longer have to huddle into one room to keep warm? Is it possible that soon there will be a toilet and a bath fitted inside every house, and that the old tin baths will only be needed to wash the dog? Is it really feasible that every home will have at least one television set, and that within a few years you will be able to watch all your favourite television programmes in colour? Can you believe that the GPO telephone boxes that are so prevalent on the streets today will some day become almost redundant? Not only will everyone have their own telephone, they will even walk around with them in their pockets! Many of these things are way

A young boy and girl enjoy a ride in their new red metal motorcar, in South London, *c.* 1962.

beyond the imagination of the average grown-up, let alone a young child. You might as well suggest that one day a man will walk on the moon!

At last, you stop scraping around inside that long-suffering eggshell; you put down your spoon and allow your mum to finish clearing away the breakfast things. Resting your back against the hard wooden uprights of your chair, you turn your gaze to the skies beyond the tightly closed sash window next to the table. You have absolutely no idea that you are witnessing the start of what is to become the most exciting decade of the twentieth century, and that, in years to come, you and every other child of the 1960s will have reason to look back on these years with great fondness. Forevermore, the decade will be referred to as the 'swinging sixties', and although future generations will experience greater lifestyle improvements than you can ever imagine, they will also fantasise about what it was like to grow up in the 1960s.

You will surely have many unforgettable personal memories of your childhood, but there are also a myriad of things that touched and influenced everyone that grew up in the sixties and evoke common memories. In the early sixties, you will have experienced some of the austere 1950s' mood that rolled over into the 1960s as part of the seamless transition between decades. After all, the older generation were not likely to forget the hard times that went before, and their long-time practice of living sparingly didn't just end at the stroke of midnight on 31 December 1959. The stories you were told of the post-war hardships and food rationing suffered by your parents and grandparents are like ancient history to you, even though food rationing only finally

ended a few years earlier, in 1954. But even the most uncaring or self-absorbed child couldn't help but see the lasting reminders of war and deprivation that were still evident in the early sixties, with many bomb ruins and bomb-damaged buildings still to be seen in towns and cities. You would regularly encounter people suffering from old war injuries, not just ex-servicemen and women, but also many innocent civilians that had been caught up in enemy bombing raids on local streets and houses. It wasn't unusual to see people in their thirties and forties, particularly men, hobbling around with the aid of a crutch or a walking stick, with some having lost limbs or been made blind during the hostilities. Back in 1957, the then Prime Minister, Harold Macmillan, caused an upset when he said, 'let us be frank about it: most of our people have never had it so good'. This remark remained etched in the minds of the fifties generation; in the 1960s it was regularly paraphrased as 'You've never had it so good', and used by grown-ups to remind children of the hardships that people suffered in previous decades. However, the cold rooms, tin baths and outside toilets had not been entirely consigned to the history books. For some people, the dearth was ongoing and improvements were only gradual.

During the early sixties, more and more high-rise blocks of flats and new housing estates were being built to replace homes that had been demolished during the government's large-scale slum clearance programme, and the once familiar landscapes in some urban and rural areas were seen to be radically changing. The new homes provided more comfortable and sanitary facilities for people that had previously occupied old run-down and overcrowded terraced houses, but they were considered by many to be characterless and

ugly, lacking the community spirit previously enjoyed in the rows of old terraced houses. Some people in tower blocks felt isolated and the kids had to adapt to a whole new way of life. But there were some benefits, such as the luxury of having modern bathrooms and hot running water, thus consigning many old kettle-filled fireside tin baths to the scrapheap.

Britain was in what was called a post-war boom period, when there seemed to be factories in every street in the country that were busy making all sorts of British goods. It was a time when British products and services were in great demand and unemployment was very low. The sixties generation had much more disposable income than their predecessors and they could afford to buy and enjoy many of the things that were previously considered to be extravagant. Up until about 1962, items like television sets and telephones were regarded as luxuries, but they soon became much more affordable to ordinary people, as did labour-saving devices like vacuum cleaners and washing machines, and by the mid-sixties these were all considered to be necessities in the home. There was little sign of 'absolute poverty', as there had been in previous decades when it was obvious that some people did not have enough money to clothe themselves or to eat an adequate diet. By the mid-sixties, a great many working-class families had seen their lifestyles improve significantly, and it could have reasonably been said that most people had 'never had it so good'!

Although cultural changes were noticeable right from the start of the sixties, in retrospect, the first couple of years were monochromatic in comparison to the rest of the decade. We were still cleansing deprivation from our lives

and ridding ourselves of all the guilt we felt for having so much more to enjoy than our parents did when they grew up in the forties and fifties. From about 1962 onwards, attitudes began to change very fast, and by the mid-sixties even the old fogies were too caught up in the mood of the sixties to reflect on the frugal times that went before. The good times had finally arrived and everything was so different to anything that had gone before. It was like someone turned on the light or fine-tuned our signal so that all of a sudden there was an explosion of colourful sound and vision.

People of all ages and social backgrounds were now taking an interest in fashion and music, and although young people set the trends, older people also began to follow them. The revolutionary changes in lifestyle were all-embracing, with children from working-class families enjoying a much better standard of living than ever before and sharing in the thrill of being at the birth of exciting new forms of entertainment and fashion. At Christmas 1961, while kids were practising the latest dance craze – the Twist – in the playground, the first signs of 'mod' fashions were starting to emerge in London. By Christmas the following year, The Beatles had made their first appearance in the pop music charts with their single *Love Me Do*, and within a few months the whole music scene had exploded into action with a procession of other Mersey groups and artists hitting the big-time, quickly followed by a contingent of new groups from London, including the Rolling Stones and the Dave Clark Five.

This was the first generation of children to take a real interest in fashionable clothing, which was probably because they were the first generation to be influenced by television,

with programmes like *Thank Your Lucky Stars*, *Top of the Pops*, and, in particular, *Ready Steady Go!* This was a must-watch Friday evening show for kids who wanted to keep up to date with all the latest music and fashion, and it was co-hosted by the much respected and admired 'Queen of the Mods', Cathy McGowan. You were completely uncool if you didn't watch it, and you had to be able to recount the whole show at school on the following Monday morning. Can you believe that a grainy black and white television programme created so much excitement back then?

Back in the fifties, many schoolgirls balanced their school hats on top of their perfectly backcombed bouffant hairdos, while the Brylcreemed quiffs of fashionable schoolboys often poked out from under the front of their school cap, much to the annoyance of schoolteachers trying to enforce strict school uniform policies. In the revolutionary sixties, kids were more reluctant than ever to conform to rigorous rules on school uniform, and were continually looking for ways to bend them. With girls, the biggest rule breaker was wearing skirts above the knee, and of course there were always some who took it too far! Sadly, for those who went to strict schools, there was often a rule that the hem of your skirt had to touch the floor when you knelt down. If it didn't, then it was too short and had to be lengthened. With boys, as in the fifties, it was their haircuts that seemed to most offend authority. But attitudes were slowly changing and by 1963 it was noticeable that older people were becoming more relaxed about modern male hairstyles; even male teachers were beginning to grow their hair. The regular shearing sessions and pudding-basin haircuts started to disappear and young boys were allowed to grow their hair

longer. It was now acceptable for a boy's hair to be touching his collar at the back; at last, short back and sides were beginning to disappear, and there was no going back.

For children, some sixties revolutionary changes were somewhat less welcome. It was nice to have parents that were 'cool', but it could also be embarrassing. All of a sudden, everywhere you looked there were mums and grannies wearing knee-high boots and brightly coloured miniskirts. Dads and granddads consigned their hats and flat caps to the dustbin and allowed their hair to grow and be styled as never before. It was embarrassing for kids to see their mums and dads turning up at the school gates dressed in trendy 'mod' clothing, and it was even worse in the late sixties when flower power and hippy fashions were all the rage. These fashion-conscious mums and dads were probably only in their twenties or thirties, but to their children they were ancient! Shouldn't your mum be snuggled up by the fire in her slippers, knitting a beige chunky cardigan for dad? And shouldn't dad be whittling some wood in the garden shed and smoking a pipe? It's not their job to be trendy, that's what youngsters do. But no. This was 'the sixties', and the sixties generation was unlike any that went before. The old rulebooks were completely discarded; everyone wanted to be part of the sixties' cultural revolution. The barriers between young and old were torn down and oldies sought to reclaim their youth.

Meanwhile, children's lifestyles were changing in other, more fundamental ways, particularly in urban areas. In the early 1960s, as in previous generations, children's main source of enjoyment was playing outside in the local streets and on the greens and wastelands or bomb ruins with their

mates. This is what their parents had done before them and they encouraged their children to do the same. It was playing outside in the fresh air that rid them of their excess energy and kept them healthy. That is where they played all the best games and had such great adventures, and importantly, it is where they became streetwise. This was all part of childhood and growing up; taking a few tumbles, getting dirty, grazing knees, having a few bumps and bruises and falling out of trees. You were more afraid to go home with a torn shirt or blouse than you were with a grazed knee or a bloody nose. Cuts and grazes would be disinfected with iodine, and the telltale sign of purple iodine was often to be seen on children's knees and elbows. The sting from the antiseptic as it was applied was often worse than the pain of the accident itself. In later years, TCP antiseptic became more popular, but it really stank. The smell followed you around for hours. There was very little mollycoddling of kids in the 1960s; once a cut or graze was cleaned up and disinfected, the wounded little soldier would be sent back out into the street to fight another battle. But, over the coming years, all of this was to change. In the early 1960s, traffic levels were still fairly low and kids were able to play happily in local streets without the hindrance of parked cars and passing traffic. The main roads only suffered from traffic problems during the morning and evening rush hours and so there was little reason for vehicles to use side streets as 'rat runs'. However, car ownership doubled between 1960 and 1970, and by about 1963 traffic problems had started to spread into the residential side streets. As the years went by and car ownership continued to increase, the streets became busier and far less safe. Those previously traffic-free

A range of typical 1960s cars can be seen benefiting from the trouble-free parking that was still possible in the mid-1960s. Note the once familiar high street store names of Woolworths and International Stores in East Street, Bridport, Dorset, *c.* 1964.

streets were quickly filled with parked vehicles and it soon became impossible for children to play their chase and ball games in the road, as they had done for generations before. Exhaust fumes from passing traffic now polluted the fresh air that was once peacefully enjoyed by babies in prams on the pavements outside their houses. Very soon, just crossing a small side road became a game of dodgem cars. The quiet local back streets, where the peace had only previously been broken by the sound of excited children playing, were now changing forever. Most of the bomb ruins and derelict

war-damaged houses had by now also been demolished, cleared and rebuilt, or at least more securely fenced in. The local streets and ruins that had been handed down to the sixties kids as their main playgrounds and 'home turf' were gradually being lost to them. Now, with the exception of a few games like hopscotch, skipping and two-balls, which could all be played on the pavements, children had to go to a park, playground or swing gardens to play safely in groups. It sounds like a better alternative to playing in the streets, but there were some disadvantages, not least the fact that they now had to share territory with other groups of kids from different neighbourhoods, and territorial fights between neighbourhood gangs became more common. It was also further to run home for treatment when you fell out of a tree.

No matter what decade you were born into, everyone can recall the long hot summer days of his or her childhood, and there were certainly some of these in the sixties. You may have been fortunate in having the open fields of the countryside or the sand dunes at the seaside as your natural playgrounds, but most kids found themselves hemmed in by houses and flats in the back streets of large cities. Wherever you grew up, to you, that was your natural environment, and you thought that yours was a normal childhood. Whatever the setting, you will have played the same games and had the same thrills and spills, whether you played British Bulldog in a rural field or on an inner-city bomb ruin, you had just as much fun and nursed just as many injuries.

By the early sixties, television had overtaken radio as the most popular form of home entertainment and children were spending much more time indoors, particularly in the

early evening when most of the children's television programmes were on air. But even with all this extra time spent
in front of the television, and in spite of all the new sixties
toys and games available to them, their appetite for outdoor
adventures had not diminished. Many of the outdoor games
had been handed down to them through the generations.
Ball games, skipping, run-outs and tag were as popular as
ever, as were mischievous games like knock-down-ginger,
but when it came to make-believe they now had even more
television and cinema heroes to imitate as they played their
swashbuckling games.

Do you remember all those 1960s television advertisements that will never again see the light of day? 'Go
to work on an egg', Esso Blue Paraffin, 'Happiness is a
Hamlet', 'Radio Rentals', 'Tick-a-Tick Timex', Opal Fruits
('made to make your mouth water'), Green Shield Stamps,
Brentford Nylons, 'A Double Diamond works wonders'
and 'all because the lady loves Milk Tray'. Many of these
advertisements were better than the programmes that they
interrupted. You can't help but remember popular and well-
known 1960s television programmes like *Blue Peter*, *Doctor
Who*, *Thunderbirds*, *Star Trek* and *Top of the Pops*, but if you
dig deep into your memory bank you will recall lots more
television programmes that you tried your hardest not to
miss when you were growing up. Children's programmes
like *Crackerjack*, *Batman*, *Stingray* and *Top Cat*. Action programmes like *Bonanza*, *77 Sunset Strip*, *Danger Man* and *The
Saint*. Dramas including *The Forsyte Saga*, *Maigret* and *The
Fugitive*. And, of course, some of the earliest British soaps
like *Emergency Ward 10*, *Crossroads* and *Coronation Street*,
which were all essential viewing. Then there were the

groundbreaking comedy shows that you sometimes had to beg to stay up and watch; shows like *The Likely Lads*, *Till Death Us Do Part*, *The Liver Birds*, *That Was The Week That Was* (aka TW3) and the inimitable *Morecambe and Wise Show*. There were also many children's television personalities that you feel you grew up with, people like Valerie Singleton, Christopher Trace, John Noakes, Peter Purves, Leslie Crowther, Peter Glaze, Johnny Morris, Tony Hart, Muriel Young and Wally Whyton; not forgetting the puppet characters Pussy Cat Willum, Ollie Beak, Fred Barker and Basil Brush. And, who could ever overlook the distinctive 'Black Country' accent of Janice Nicholls on *Thank Your Lucky Stars*, with her familiar catchphrase: 'Oi'll give it foive.' These are just a few of the television memories that surely still linger in the back of your mind.

By 1964, the sixties music and fashion revolution was well under way, but the BBC was playing far too little pop music, and the only way that kids in Britain could be sure to hear the latest pop record releases was by tuning into Radio Luxembourg on 208 metres medium wave. But Luxembourg only transmitted at night-time and reception was very poor in many areas of the country. Radio Luxembourg's sound regularly faded in and out, and you had to endlessly fiddle with the tuning knob on your transistor radio to pick up the signal. However, all of this changed on Easter Sunday 1964 when the then little-known actor and disc jockey Simon Dee made the first broadcast from the offshore 'pirate' radio station, Radio Caroline. The music revolution had well and truly begun when, for the first time ever, you could listen to pop music all day long. Soon, several other 'pirate' radio stations were broadcasting from various coastal and offshore

locations around Britain, allowing access to endless amounts of pop music for kids all across the country. No longer would you be forced to endure BBC radio programmes like *The Billy Cotton Band Show* or *Desert Island Discs*: Radio would never be the same again.

Your schooldays may now be just a distant memory, but there are things you encounter in your everyday life that can suddenly take you back there. It could be a smell that reminds you of your old school bag, a textbook or the inside of your old pencil case. Perhaps there is an unpleasant odour that reminds you of the lingering pong around a pile of sand that the school caretaker once left in the corridor outside your old classroom; maybe the smell of boiled cabbage reminds you of all those lovely school dinners you once tried so hard to avoid. In autumn, when you see horse chestnut tree seed pods lying split open on the ground and revealing shiny new brown conkers, you might, for a moment, be tempted to collect them all up as you did back in your schooldays when you used to play conkers with your mates in the playground. Just planting sweet peas around canes in the garden will be enough to stir the memory of anyone who was ever at the wrong end of a caning when they were at school in the 1960s, long before corporal punishment was abolished.

You will have enjoyed playing with so many new toys, more than any generation before. Advancements in plastic manufacturing techniques during the fifties meant that the 1960s plastic toys could be made in all shapes and sizes, in bright colours and with smoothly rounded edges. The toy industry began to mass-produce metal and plastic toys in response to the huge demand that was being created from

new television programmes like *Doctor Who and Daleks* and *Thunderbirds*, and by cinema heroes like James Bond. Also, children were starting to be greatly influenced by the promotion of new toys through television advertising, such as Sindy Doll and Action Man. All sorts of games and toys could now be bought at affordable prices. Boys' old cowboy cap guns were soon replaced with new toy space guns, and girls' trusty but staid old toy dolls were upgraded to new highly fashionable talking dolls with interchangeable fashion accessories. Children's toy boxes and cupboards were quickly filled with all sorts of new toys, from pogo sticks to space buggies.

Children and adults enjoy a ride on the small road train and in chair lifts at Butlins Holiday Camp in Filey, Yorkshire, *c.* 1965.

The way we took our holidays and the destinations began to change. The traditional seaside, bucket and spade, stick of rock and kiss-me-quick hat sort of holidays were still very popular, but access to many of the smaller seaside and rural holiday destinations was becoming increasingly difficult by train, and the old romantic notion of a holiday train journey was turning into a thing of the past. From 1950–62, over 3,000 miles of British railway lines had been closed for various reasons, and in 1962, the then chairman of British Railways, Dr Richard Beeching, instigated what was called the 'Beeching axe', which resulted in the shutting down of a further 4,000 miles of railway and the closure of 3,000 stations in the period from 1963–72. More modern diesel and electric trains were replacing the old steam locomotives, but the reduced train services coupled with increasing car ownership meant that more and more people were now travelling to the seaside by car rather than train. However, that same age-old question could still be heard, only now it was coming from the back seat of a car: 'Are we nearly there?' But the familiar British seaside resorts were no longer the only holiday destinations. There was an extra added bonus of growing up in the 1960s, in that you were the first generation of children to experience the luxury of foreign travel. The new charter airlines enabled ordinary people to take 'cheap package holidays' to exotic foreign destinations – to go abroad, just like film stars and royalty.

On a sourer note, it was a time when even children were aware that the world was in danger from dreadful wars, particularly in the early sixties with all the talk of the Cuban Missile Crisis and the possibility of nuclear war, with constant references to the Cold War and the 'four-

minute warning'. We heard much talk about Britain's secret observatories at Jodrell Bank and Fylingdales, but we didn't really understand what it was all about. We were apparently all under threat from this strange, mysterious place called the Soviet Union. Do you remember trying to work out what you would do in those final four minutes if the warning ever came? There was great rivalry in the school playground to see who could come up with the most outrageous thing possible, but, unfortunately, most of the ideas required more than four minutes, and of course you couldn't plan for where you would be when the four-minute warning was given. There were also the regular news reports and general talk about the ongoing Vietnam War, and although Britain was not directly involved in the war, we saw all the chilling newspaper headlines and television coverage of the anti-war and 'ban the bomb' marches. The shock of President Kennedy's assassination in 1963 didn't escape children either, with everyone talking about it at home, on the streets and at school. It was a scary time, with schoolboys fearful that, at best, the government would bring back conscription and they would be called up to join the armed forces and fight in wars when they left school. As in every decade, there were some serious world issues to concentrate everyone's minds, and for students to protest about. But, having said that, there were plenty of good things going on to distract us from the more sombre issues; an overwhelming abundance of exciting new experiences to celebrate and enjoy. There were so many 'firsts' in the sixties: the first time you saw an E-Type Jaguar, the first time you watched colour television and the first time England won the football World Cup. You

will never forget the first episode of *Doctor Who*, the first Beatles record you ever heard or the first magazine picture you saw of Twiggy in a miniskirt.

It wasn't just the kids that were influenced by the ever-increasing slick American-style television advertising on ITV. Our cupboards and medicine cabinets were beginning to bulge with products we had been convinced to buy through television advertisements. Accordingly, mums kept more medicinal treatments for minor ailments in their bathroom cabinets at home. Strong-smelling antiseptics, like Germoline and TCP, were popular for treating little warriors' cuts and grazes; after all, if it had a strong smell, then it must be good. Such pungent antiseptic smells were associated with the mix of ether and other aromas that permeated hospital corridors, and this provided extra comfort that these products were good for treating wounded children. Kids acquired lots of cuts and bruises, but were generally very fit because of all those exhausting and dangerous outdoor games they played; nevertheless, they still couldn't escape the childhood illnesses. Chicken Pox, Measles, Whooping Cough, German Measles, Mumps and Tonsillitis: they got them all!

Do you remember those huge needles that the doctor used to stick into your arm as a child, and the anxiety you felt as you queued at school or in some draughty church hall to be inoculated against diseases like Diphtheria, TB (Tuberculosis) and Polio? The reassuring words passed on to you by other kids that had gone before, like 'It was a really big needle!' and 'It really hurt!' just made you feel so much better. This was a time when, if you were ill, you didn't need to make an appointment to see your doctor; you just turned

up at the surgery during surgery hours and waited your turn. Doctors' waiting rooms were small, intimate places, simply furnished with rows of upright hardback wooden chairs. There was usually no receptionist to manage the patients and most doctors would retrieve patients' notes from filing cabinets themselves. Apart from the wooden chairs, the only accessory in the waiting room was often just a bell or buzzer for the doctor to summon the next patient. Some doctors didn't even have one of those; they would rely on an exiting patient to send in the next person. Doctors did a lot of home visits; if your mum said you were ill in bed, the doctor came out without any fuss, even in the middle of the night or at the weekend. It all seemed very efficient and free of bureaucracy.

Dental treatment improved during the 1960s, but a visit to the dentist was still something to dread, especially for those unfortunate enough to have experienced the gas anaesthetic dentistry of the early sixties. It was the stuff of nightmares. That horrible cube of dry wadding that the dentist would shove under your back teeth to keep your mouth open and the awful smell of the black rubber face mask that was held over your nose and mouth to administer the anaesthetic gas that would send you to sleep and into a world of hallucinatory nightmarish dreams. Afterwards, you drifted back into consciousness tasting the disgusting mix of bleeding gums and residual gas in your mouth, and the nausea inevitably brought on bouts of uncontrollable vomiting. The horrendous experience didn't end at the dentist's door because the soreness, nausea and dizziness could last for several hours. Who could question why a child of the sixties would often need to be dragged screaming and

Children play with their buckets and spades on the beach at Hayling Island in Hampshire, *c.* 1961.

shouting to the dentist's chair? The ever-increasing use of local anaesthetic injections was much more tolerable, but even so, the needles were not as good as they are today, and yes, they did hurt.

Any child that was hospitalised in the 1960s will remember the Nightingale wards, named after Florence Nightingale, with rows of beds each side of a long room and large tables in the middle where the nurses did their paperwork and held meetings. The nurses were always so clean and smart in their uniform, with white starched bib-front pinafore dresses and caps, and blue elasticated belts with a crest on the buckle. Most had an upside-down watch pinned to the top of their pinafore for use when they checked patients' pulses. The smell of ether was always present throughout hospital buildings, but if you were an inpatient you soon got used to it. There were always loads of bicycles parked in hospital courtyards; every nurse and young doctor seemed to have one. Up until the late sixties, NHS hospitals were run very formally, with Matron's daily inspections sending every nurse into a panic, but you were very well looked after – and the doctors and nurses were wonderful.

Looking back on that very first morning of 1960, when you were sitting at the breakfast table eating your soft-boiled egg and pondering what the day might have in store for you, could you have possibly ever dreamed of the wonders you would experience over the next few years? A childhood journey that was to take you from crayons to felt-tip pens, gymslips to miniskirts, snake belts to kaftans, *Janet and John* to *The Godfather* and from Margate to Benidorm. All of your earliest memories are sandwiched

between these, and whatever age you were by the end of the sixties, whether you were still drawing geometric shapes with your Spirograph or listening to Bob Dylan at the Isle of Wight music festival, you will surely have seen improvements to your own overall lifestyle and witnessed at least some of the major cultural changes of the sixties. This was a special decade, in which everything seemed to convert from monochrome to colour. It is hard to believe that so much happened in so few years.

Two

HOME LIFE

It's very early in the morning on Saturday 17 July 1965. This is the first day of the school holidays and you are tucked up in your warm bed dreaming of how you will spend the next six weeks of freedom. The weather has been improving over the last few days and the forecast for the coming week is good. You are awake but you haven't yet opened your eyes, instead preferring to snuggle beneath the sheets and delay the start of your day for as long as possible. It was a bit chilly overnight, but you managed to create a nice warm cocoon under the heavy blankets that pin you to the mattress and shield you from drafts. You can hear the faint sound of music coming from the radio downstairs, and can just about decipher the song as being *Mr Tambourine Man* by The Byrds. You begin to accept the inevitable dawning

of a new day, and in doing so you allow your mind to fully focus on the tune that is filtering through the closed bedroom door. Instinctively humming along to the melody, you now find yourself fighting to free your arms from the weight of the bedclothes so that you can strum an imaginary twelve-string jangling guitar in time with the music. By now you are fully awake and venture to slightly open one eye to welcome in the day. The early morning sunlight is streaming through the thin cotton curtains and projecting a beam of light onto the Bob Dylan poster that is stuck to the wall next to your bed. The curtains are completely useless at keeping out the daylight and serve only to deny prying eyes. Still scanning the room with the one half-open eye, you turn your head and lift it slightly off the pillow so that you can see the time on the bedside alarm clock. It's only just approaching half-past seven, but the welcoming sunlight provides you with enough courage to bravely creep out from under your blanket-laden cocoon. With both eyes now fully open, you lift yourself up onto one elbow, throw back the bedcovers, and slide your body nearer to the edge of the bed. Having swung your legs over the side of the bed and settled both feet on the floor, you stretch your upper body and rub the sleep from your eyes before lifting yourself up and making your way over to the window to pull back the curtains, flooding the room with daylight. The sudden movement has provoked extra pressure on your bladder and you are now desperate for the loo. You quickly skip around your prized Dansette record player and a pile of records in the middle of the floor, but can't avoid stepping on a neglected purple-haired troll doll as you make your way out of the bedroom and down the

hall to the bathroom. On the way, your ears are filled with the fabulous sounds of jangling guitars and melodic harmonies that are wafting up the stairs at full volume. Thank goodness for Radio Caroline!

While sitting on the toilet, you unroll a few sheets of the Izal soft toilet tissue and revel in its luxury, thinking back to just a few months earlier when mum was still forcing you to use those shiny, slippery, individually folded thin sheets of Izal medicated toilet paper that came in a small cardboard box dispenser. They weren't absorbent enough and were really uncomfortable and messy to use. You needed to use about a dozen sheets, and even that wasn't enough to do the job properly; mind you, it did serve as a useful alternative to tracing paper when drawing pictures. Continuing to ponder away the time, you reflect on how fortunate you are to be sitting on this modern toilet when several of your friends are still having to make do with outside lavatories, and some even have to share an outside lavvy with their neighbours. Outside lavvys are quite scary places for kids, usually dark, damp and draughty old lean-tos at the back of houses, with the chilling sound of dripping water echoing from inside high-level cisterns and condensation running down exposed pipes – reminiscent of the lavatory blocks in school playgrounds.

Still seated on your comfortable loo, you lean over the bath to examine the removeable rubber shower hose that has been left attached to the bath taps, and you wonder at the ingenuity of someone inventing such a thing. Wouldn't it be great if you could have a proper shower, like in the shower blocks at holiday camps or, better still, like the posh ones you see all the time in Hollywood films?

Having made best use of the soft toilet tissue and then flushed it all away, you stand for a moment to admire the pink fluffy toilet-seat cover with its matching cut-out rug at the base of the toilet pan. Then, turning your gaze to the uninviting bare bits of linoleum floor, you swiftly hop across to the other pink rug beneath the sink and nestle your bare feet into its deep fluffy pile. Even in summer, the exposed areas of linoleum floors are really cold. The new fluffy set-of-three are welcome additions to the bathroom and they look rather posh too. Mum really is quite a trendsetter.

Turning on the hot tap, as always, the 'boom' from the Ascot gas water heater above the sink surprises you as it sparks into life and its chamber fills with flames, creaking away noisily as the whole contraption heats up and expands. While splashing the water around in the sink, you move things about on the shelf next to you to see if there is anything of interest there. There are bottles of Alka-Seltzer, Milk of Magnesia and Eno Fruit Salts, and at the end of the shelf is a collection of women's make-up, including a packet of false eyelashes, some mascara and a white lipstick, which seems to be all the rage. Nothing very exciting. But look! Mum's bought some of that new Signal toothpaste with the pink stripes that they've been advertising on the telly. You quickly grab hold of the tube and squeeze some of its stripy toothpaste onto your toothbrush. Umm, yes … it's quite nice, and it must be good for your teeth because, like they said on the television, it has these special pink stripes running all the way through it.

Having finished in the bathroom, you go back to your bedroom to get dressed, leaving the bedroom door ajar so you can hear the downstairs radio and immerse yourself

in Phil Spector's *Wall of Sound* bellowing the Righteous Brothers' song, *You've Lost That Loving Feeling*, all round the house.

A lovely sunny day – t-shirt, blue jeans and sneakers will do – now, downstairs for breakfast and then off to the Odeon cinema and Saturday Morning Pictures with all your mates.

Around the House

Whereas the older generation had been satisfied to surround themselves with fairly modest personal belongings, and content to furnish their homes with post-war utility furniture, the young and more affluent homemakers of the sixties were looking to replace all the heavy dark-wooden furniture with more modern streamline styles, like those being sold in the newly opened Habitat stores. The do-it-yourself home improvement fad did not arrive in Britain until the 1970s, but during the 1960s people all over the country found enough enthusiasm to search in under-stair cupboards and garden sheds to find some basic tools so that they could do their small bit towards modernising the inside of their homes to match the clean lines of sixties-style furnishings. The average 1960s DIY project usually involved the use of a large hammer and loads of nails. The entire modernisation project mostly entailed boxing in ornate fireplaces and stair rails, and boarding up interior doors to produce smooth clean-cut surfaces. Today, these crude and amateur DIY practices are frowned upon, and in recent years the popularity of DIY restoration work has resulted

in many of these old boxed-in treasures being uncovered to reveal some wonderful fireplaces, staircases and panelled doors. By the mid-sixties, many houses were filled with a mismatch of old and new furnishings, so people were all too quickly disposing of their old-fashioned dark-wood furniture and what they saw as tasteless heirloom clocks, mirrors, pictures and ornaments. You probably watched eagerly from the sidelines as your parents gradually rid the house of all that horrible old granny stuff, and replaced it with new-generation lightweight furniture with sticky-out matchstick legs and modern accessories. Little did you know that in years to come, as an adult, you would spend hours and perhaps days at a time traipsing around antique fairs and shops looking to acquire some of those same 'old granny' items that, as a child, you happily encouraged mum and dad to throw out. Yes, you could never have imagined that what you once considered to be horrible, old-fashioned, ugly has-beens would one day be much sought after by collectors, and many of those discarded heirlooms would even be credibly tagged as valuable antiques, for which you would eagerly fork out your hard-earned cash and bring back to fill the rooms and shelves in your twenty-first-century home. All of your old toys and books that were binned, and even that old upright piano that once had pride of place in your parents' front room, how you wish you had held on to them; if only you had known.

The cosy comfort that you enjoyed when snuggling up close to an open fire in wintertime was, for many, becoming a thing of the past, with fancy new gas fires and two-bar electric fires being fitted onto the front of newly boxed-in fireplaces, replacing the old solid fuel burning grates. This

was the sixties and the main focal point of a room was no longer its fireplace and the gentle hypnotic flames of an open fire. While the newly boxed-in fireplace still provided the main heating in the room, the seating was now strategically positioned so that the whole family could get a good view of the television. New, stylish radiograms and transistor radios were gradually replacing the trusty old wireless valve radio cabinets that used to sit on top of the sideboard, purring soft mesmerising tones right across the room. The radiogram usually took pride of place in the front room, or parlour as they were sometimes called. The front room housed all the best furniture and was usually reserved for special occasions, like Christmas or when you had visitors. In reality, these front or 'best' rooms were just dust harbours and a complete waste of space. They hardly ever got used because visitors usually preferred to sit in an everyday back room or the kitchen, both being more lived-in, warm and cosy.

Although electric clocks had been around for many years, the sound of ticking clocks was still prevalent in 1960s homes, with most people choosing to stick with the old faithful wind-up clocks, which were much cheaper. It was quite normal to have clocks all around the house, all sorts of clocks in every room, even in the hallway, and all showing slightly different times. Today, kids would probably find the rhythmic ticking of a bedroom clock an unbearable sound to contend with in the still of the night, but they used to be just part of the furniture and you somehow didn't even notice them. Mind you, if you were progressive enough to have electric clocks in the 1960s then you would have needed to find spare electrical sockets to plug them

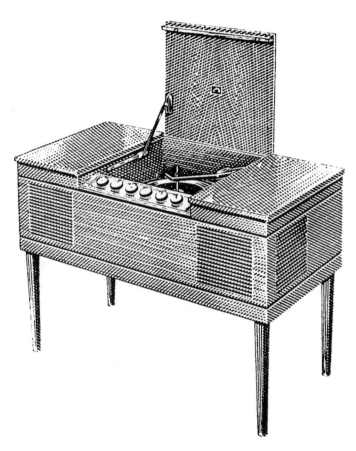

This was the very latest HMV Stereomaster radiogram, and anyone would have been proud to have it pride of place in their living room in 1966.

in, and that could be a big problem. In many homes there was a shortage of electric wall sockets and the recent arrival of all the new electrical household items frequently over-whelmed the old domestic electrical circuits. Most rooms only had one electric wall socket and these were already overloaded with multiple add-on three-socket adapters in every room. Using these adapters, several electrical items were often plugged into one single wall socket. All those plugs, with their tangled spaghetti of wires hanging down from the wall, going off in all directions round the room to power such things as the television set, record player, porta-ble heater, hairdryer and lamps. People didn't seem to realise how dangerous it was. Every now and then there would be a frightening flash and an almighty bang when the over-loaded electrical circuit would blow fuses in the plugs and in the main fuse box, leaving the house in darkness.

Fully fitted carpets became fashionable in the 1960s, and gradually more and more of them were being fitted into the average home, but mainly in the living room, with rugs and sheet lino or lino tiles still evident all round the rest of the house. The thought of losing that strip of bare lino round the edge of the old carpet was a sad loss to any child that had experienced the thrill of sliding along it in stockinged feet. Also, some of the new fitted carpets might not have been as comfortable as expected. If you had the misfortune of having a bri-nylon carpet, then you will, no doubt, have experienced a few static electric shocks when running around the carpet in your stockings, particularly if your mum was in the habit of kitting you out in bri-nylon clothes – then the sparks would really begin to fly. Ugh, those horrible nylon shirts, blouses, slips and even knick-

ers. And worst of all, going to bed in your nylon nightie or pyjamas, and being frightened to move in case you rubbed against the nylon sheets and made sparks – every night was like bonfire night. Then, in the morning, you would be all clammy and the nylon would be clinging to you like wet glue. Horrible!

If you were blessed with anything larger than a galley kitchen, then it was probably regarded as the hub of the home, where everyone congregated. The kitchen table was often used as a multitask workbench, providing a platform for everything from bathing the baby to doing your home-work on. By the mid-sixties, the old 'whistle kettles', which used to be permanent fixtures on top of the stove, had been replaced by modern electric kettles and the age-old tradi-tion of boiling endless supplies of water to keep a fresh pot of tea on the go was only occasionally interrupted when dad changed a blown fuse in the plug. There was a clear dividing line between what was regarded as a man or woman's job around the house, and changing fuses was one of dad's jobs. It was a time when dads did the more 'manly' jobs around the house (before the age of the 'modern man'); things like decorating, gardening and fixing things, basically anything that involved using a hammer, spanner, spade or ladder. Mums were expected to look after the children and do most of the routine domestic chores. They were still tagged as being housewives, even if they went out to work as well. It was traditional for young girls to be taught cooking, baking, knitting and sewing as part of their essential learning, while boys were taught the more industrial skills of woodwork and metalwork. Women boasted that the kitchen was part of their domain and men were discouraged from interfering

with anything that went on in there. Unsurprisingly, most men happily followed this rule to the letter.

The revival of 'women's lib' did not succeed in removing the shackles of domesticity from most mums' lives, but looking after the home was no longer as labour intensive and hard work as it had been for previous generations. The benefits of having electrically powered domestic appliances, like washing machines, fridges, freezers, sewing machines and vacuum cleaners, meant that women were no longer slaves to the home. Having fridges and freezers meant that they could now go shopping once a week rather than every day for fresh food, as they had before. Many households now had use of a car and people could get about more easily, making 'nipping to the shops' a much simpler task than previously, and there were no severe parking restrictions as there are now – you could actually park outside a shop without the risk of being fined by a council official or by Dodgy & Co. wheel clampers. People found that they had more free time to enjoy life. It wasn't all work, work and more work, like it had been in the past.

The old-style scullery kitchens of yesteryear, with shelf and under-sink storage and food pantries, were gradually being replaced by fitted kitchens. Nothing as grand as is available today, but kitchens were being smartened up as never before, and space was being created to accommodate all of the new kitchen gadgets that were now becoming commonplace; things like electric toasters, pedal bins, food mixers, wall-mounted can openers, coffee percolators, lightweight scales, electric carving knives and, if your mum and dad were really 'with it', then they would have needed somewhere to display that fancy new fondue set.

Unfortunately, microwave ovens and dishwashers didn't find their way into British kitchens until the seventies and eighties. The traditional kitchen equipment, by now regarded as laborious and old fashioned, was consigned to the scrapheap, and granny's cumbersome old mangle and washboard were dumped outside the back door to await the rag-and-bone man's next visit. All of those famous old brand names, previously so visible around the kitchen, like Omo, Vim, Ajax, Brillo, Windolene, Ibcol, Brasso and Robin Starch, were now hidden away behind smart new cabinet doors.

Smoking was very popular in the sixties and most adults seemed to smoke cigarettes, cigars or a pipe. It was not unusual to find ashtrays in every room of the house, even in the bedrooms. The main sitting room often had a floor-standing ashtray with a handle on top so that it could be moved round the room. People carried all sorts of differently designed cigarette lighters around with them, but it was also quite common to have a large, fancy table lighter somewhere in the main living room, usually sitting on the coffee table or on the fireplace mantle shelf. All of the soft furnishings must have reeked with the smell of cigarette and pipe smoke, not to mention people's hair and clothes, but the smell of stale cigarette smoke was always there, everywhere you went, and somehow you didn't even notice it. In summer, you could open all the windows to refresh the air in the house, but in the cold of winter the best that you could do was to spray the rooms with a can of air freshener. Many a house fire was started by emptying ashtrays into a kitchen bin without noticing a smouldering cigarette hidden among the pile of dog-ends. For most people

in the sixties, a house fire was considered to be about the only way that smoking could seriously damage your health or kill you. Smoking was still considered to be 'cool' back then, and there were no restrictions on cigarette advertising, nor were there any health warnings on packets. It was very easy for children to buy cigarettes, and many young kids smoked secretly with their mates, starting from as young as 10 years old.

Food and Drink

As with many things in the 1960s, there was an enormous change in children's attitudes towards food and drink from one end of the decade to the other. In the early sixties, kids generally ate what they were given because their parents were still preaching the 1950s' 'be grateful for what you have' message of austerity, but television advertising was really starting to influence everyone, not least the kids, and parents were finding it increasingly hard to resist the pressures to buy all sorts of foods and drinks that were being heavily advertised. The clever slogans and jingles that they used really did work, and you would nag your mum to buy the products that appeared in the most memorable advertisements, even if those products weren't meant for kids. You just couldn't get the jingles out of your head, and they are surely still firmly fixed in your mind today. Everyone remembers them: 'A million housewives everyday, pick up a can of beans and say, Beanz Meanz Heinz'; 'Murray Mints, Murray Mints, too good to hurry mints'; 'Now hands that do dishes can feel soft as your face, with mild green Fairy

Liquid'; 'A Double Diamond works wonders, so drink one today!'; When you fancy a fruity treat ... Unzip a Banana!'; 'Opal Fruits (made to make your mouth water)'; 'The Milkybar kid is strong and tough, and only the best is good enough – Nestlé's Milkybar'; 'You'll look a little lovelier each day, with fabulous pink Camay' (with Katie Boyle) and 'Hovis, the golden heart of a meal'. There were so many familiar brand names that regularly flashed across our television screens, including Birds Eye, Findus and Ross Frozen Food, Cadbury's Smash, Cheerios cereal, Winalot dog food, Kraft Dairylea cheese, Crosse & Blackwell soups, Huntley & Palmer biscuits, Rose's lime juice, Wall's sausages, Chiver's jellies, HP sauce, Robinson's barley water (especially during Wimbledon week), the Cadbury's 'man in black' (all because the lady loves Milk Tray) and the Nimble balloon girl (Maggie). It was Esso that 'put a tiger in your tank' and it was Tony Hancock and Patricia Hayes that reminded us all that we should 'Go to work on an egg!' We were bombarded with brand names like never before – Britvic, Ribena, Horlicks, Bovril – there were so many and we wanted them all.

As the years went by, kids were spending more and more time indoors in the early evening, watching television rather than playing outside. However, the computer age was still a long way off and kids remained very active, playing outside as much as possible. It was considered important to have three square meals a day. Breakfast was usually cereal (Snap, Crackle and Pop – Kellogg's Rice Krispies were preferred) or porridge or a lightly boiled egg with bread soldiers to dip in it. A full breakfast or 'fry-up' was reserved for the weekend, when breakfast became a real meal, with egg,

Typical of early 1960s advertisements. This one is offering an affordable
portable tape recorder and a children's slide, both on easy terms, c. 1962.

bacon, sausage, tomatoes, baked beans, black pudding and fried bread. We had never heard of cholesterol back then, so everything except the baked beans was fried. Coffee was becoming more and more popular, but tea was still first choice for most people, so there was always a fresh pot of tea available.

For main meals there were lots of stews and homemade meat pies, always with loads of potatoes and vegetables. Frozen foods were becoming increasingly popular and so not everything was as fresh as in earlier years. You were always made to eat everything on your plate – 'eat your greens up or you won't grow' and 'eat your carrots or you won't be able to see in the dark'. Every Sunday you had a traditional roast dinner in the early afternoon, with chicken, roast beef, pork or lamb and roast potatoes with lots of vegetables and gravy. Sunday's leftovers were served up on Monday and Tuesday in the form of stew, meat pie or cold meat dishes. During the rest of the week, you would have a variety of wholesome dishes for dinner, including liver and bacon, bangers and mash, lamb or pork chops, egg and chips, toad-in-the-hole, bubble and squeak and the traditional fish and chips on Fridays.

We were also starting to acquire a taste for foreign cuisine, due mainly to an increasing amount of foreign travel, which introduced us to dishes like spaghetti bolognese; and there were growing numbers of Indian and Chinese takeaway restaurants, not forgetting the fast nationwide spread of the American chain of Colonel Sanders' Kentucky Fried Chicken, now known as KFC, takeaway food shops. The Wimpy bars' chain of fast-food restaurants was already well established, and in the 1960s they were *the* place to

go for hamburgers. Sadly, British kids had to wait until 1974 before they could experience their first McDonald's hamburger. But, through it all, fish and chips remained the nation's favourite dish.

In summer, there were boring cold meat salads to contend with, only made tolerable by drowning everything in salad cream. Thinly sliced pieces of Spam would often be found haunting the salad plate. Spam was one of those mystery processed meats, supposedly made mostly from pork, but it had a strange taste and texture that didn't appeal much to kids and was often found hidden under some left-over lettuce after a salad meal.

The practice of eating food in front of the television from a plate that was sliding around on a melamine tray balanced precariously on your lap was not yet the custom. Most families adopted the tradition of the whole family sitting down together at the table for meals, and usually at specific times. But, as always, kids could be picky eaters, and they would sometimes select favourite bits of food from their dinner plate to eat as a sandwich and then push the rest of the dinner to one side; mashed potatoes or chips stuffed between two slices of bread would often be more desirable to them than having to eat the whole meal that their mum had painstakingly cooked for them. Other popular kids' sandwiches included salad cream, jam, banana, cheese, fish paste and, of course, beef or pork dripping – mmm, bread and dripping – lov-e-ly! Dripping was the product of fat and liquid that was left in the pan after mum had cooked a joint of beef or pork. Kids loved the taste of it and fish and chips cooked in beef dripping were just delicious – yet another joy of not knowing about cholesterol.

Puddings, sweets or 'afters', as they were often called, were usually a luxury reserved for Sundays, after your Sunday roast dinner. Rice pudding, bread and butter pudding and semolina or tapioca milk puddings – you either loved them or hated them. Homemade spotted dick or apple pie served with Bird's yellow custard with the skin on top, or if you were really posh you might have pink blancmange. Pineapple chunks with Carnation milk, jelly and ice cream, trifle and the occasional luxury of a block of Neapolitan ice cream.

Tradesmen and Services

Right up until the end of the 1960s, there were a lot of homes that were only just having their very first telephone installed. Some telephone exchanges couldn't cope with the ever-increasing demand for home telephones and you often had to wait months for a phone to be installed. Even then, many households had to make do with having only a shared or party-line, which meant that two or more subscribers shared the same pair of wires and only one party could make a call at a time. It was a terrible service, and neighbours could listen in on each other's phone calls. Before you could make a call, you had to press a button on top of the phone to signal the exchange that you were about to do so and that you should be billed for it. If you wanted to make a phone call when the other party was already using the line, then you had to wait until they had finished. If you needed to make an emergency call then you had to tell the other party to get off the line. For obvious reasons, there was no

such thing as telesales or telemarketing in the 1960s, which was good. The only telephone calls you got were from people you knew. Simply bliss! Also, there were no computers to compile lists of addresses for direct mail companies to bombard you with mountains of junk mail. But businesses did have to get their message across somehow, and so there were a lot of door-to-door salesmen and tallymen selling goods on the never-never. *Encyclopaedia Britannica* salesmen were very active at the time, selling their 24-volume set of encyclopaedias door-to-door on easy payment terms. They struck fear into the heart of every timid young parent who wanted their children to do well at school. After all, your child had no hope of passing their 11-plus or GCE exams if they didn't have access to their very own set of *Encyclopaedia Britannica*, and the books did look stunning. Our parents just weren't used to the American style of 'hard sell'.

It seems like an ancient bygone age now, but it was a time when postmen still wore a smart head-to-toe uniform with collar and tie, highly polished black leather shoes and a flat 'military style' peaked cap. It would have been inconceivable for them to wear trainers and shorts back then. The post always dropped through the letterbox at about 7 a.m. each day, with the second post arriving at about 11 a.m., or did we just imagine that?

We still had a telegram service with telegram boys delivering about 10 million telegrams a year. Other than by telephone, a telegram was the fastest way to get a message to someone, but they were expensive to send and were usually only used to relay urgent messages. Telegrams were traditionally sent to announce the birth of a child or to congratulate a newly married couple, but an unexpected

telegram was frequently carrying bad news, more often than not advising the recipient of a serious illness or the death of a friend or family member. Nobody liked to see a telegram boy coming along their street, and people would breathe a big sigh of relief when he carried on past their house. The young telegram boys, in their navy blue uniforms with red piping and pillbox caps, were a familiar sight, especially in urban areas, but numbers were gradually reducing with more and more messages being delivered by telephone and telex. Fax machines were still a long way off and emails were decades away.

Throughout the sixties it was still common practice to have your milk delivered fresh to your doorstep each morning. Virtually every area had a milk roundsman, and as with most delivery men back then, the milkman wore a uniform, including a collar and tie and a peaked cap, with a lightweight protective jacket or overall, and some also wore an apron. By the mid-sixties, most large dairies were using electric milk floats for their daily doorstep deliveries, but many of the small local dairies were still using handcarts or horse-drawn carts. In rural areas, it wasn't unusual to see milk carts being pulled by a farm tractor. Each evening your mum would put all of your empty milk bottles (washed, of course) out on the doorstep for the milkman to collect the next day when he delivered your fresh milk. Everyone had a regular standing order, but if you wanted to change your milk order or needed to add some dairy products or orange juice to the next day's order, then your mum would leave a note for the milkman in one of the empties. The milkmen would start their rounds very early in the morning and so the milk

would arrive on most people's doorsteps while they were still tucked up in bed. It meant fresh milk for breakfast, but people would often grumble that the noise from clinking milk bottles and the clattering of metal milk crates disturbed their sleep and woke them up far too early. Oh, and milkmen always seemed to be whistling unrecognisable tunes – loudly! In outlying areas, people would often have groceries and bread delivered to their door by van, and it was quite usual for the delivery roundsmen to be offered several cups of tea en route.

Once a week the dustmen would come to collect the dustbin full of rubbish. It now seems amazing that the rubbish accumulated by a whole family would only fill one small metal dustbin. There was very little unnecessary packaging to dispose of and there was hardly any waste food. The dustmen would collect the dustbin from wherever it was normally kept, be it in the back garden or in a side alley, but most people did put them outside the back gate or next to the front door, ready for collection on the prescribed day. There were no bureaucratic rules for the disabled and old people to worry about.

By the mid-sixties, many households were using electric or gas for their heating, but there remained a lot of open fires in regular use, which meant there was still a demand for local coal deliveries. The coal was usually delivered on motorised flatbed lorries, but there were still some horse-drawn drays around. The coalmen were usually large, intimidating men with faces and hands blackened by coal dust. They often wore flat caps and sleeveless leather jackets. The coalmen would heave the huge hundredweight (cwt) sacks of coal off the flatbed lorry and carry them on their

backs to the coalbunkers, or tip them through a coalhole in the pavement into the cellar below.

Mums hated it when the chimney sweep came to clean the chimney. Some chimney sweeps had small vans, but many were still using pushbikes to get around – riding along with the aid of just one hand while supporting a few long-handled brushes on their shoulder with the other. The sweep would have a permanent covering of soot all over, even when he had just arrived. All the furniture would be pushed back from the fireplace and covered with sheets, but it was always a nerve-wracking experience for house-proud mums. For the kids, it was amusing to watch the expression on mum's face as the sweep manoeuvred his brushes up the chimney and a cloud of soot bellowed out from beneath the protective sheet, dispensing a nice covering of black dust around the room. The sweep would always be carefully escorted from the house when he had finished, making sure that he didn't rub up against anything he passed on the way. Then the clean-up would begin.

Window cleaners were also beginning to change their mode of transport from old-fashioned pushbikes to small vans, but many of the steadfast pushbike users still carried their stepladder and bucket in a homemade wooden box attached to the side of their bike, just like a motorbike sidecar.

More and more people were switching from the pay-as-you-go shilling-in-the-slot gas and electric meters to, instead, paying an invoice or bill. The gas and electric meter readers still called regularly to take meter readings, but you no longer got an immediate cash refund for the amount that the pay-as-you-go meter had overcharged (these meters were set to overcharge and so there was always a refund).

Three

OUT ON THE STREETS

It's Whit Saturday morning, 16 May 1964, and in the high street there are hundreds of excited kids standing outside the Odeon cinema waiting for the doors to open for their weekly session of children's films and live entertainment. Some are looking at the still pictures from the new war film, *633 Squadron*, which are displayed on the wall outside the cinema, while others are practising their yo-yoing skills ahead of the yo-yo contest that will take place during the interval. As more and more kids arrive, the queue becomes increasingly disordered and spreads out across the pavement, making it difficult for people to get by without stepping into the road or weaving their way through the noisy crowd of youngsters. One of the older boys lets out a loud wolf-whistle in admiration of two miniskirt-clad teenage girls

walking along the pavement on the other side of the road. Their miniskirts are actually micro skirts that are so short they could easily be mistaken for belts. The girls smile and blush with embarrassment as they look across the road and realise that their admirer is just a pasty-faced 12-year-old boy. A spontaneous collective cheer of delight goes up from a group of queuing boys as they see the two girls react with obvious discomfort at the unwanted attention they are getting. As if in haste to escape a thousand ogling eyes, the girls quickly enter through the doors of the adjacent C&A store and disappear from view. A few minutes later, a large convoy of motor-scooters drive past, briefly replacing the more usual high street traffic noise with the combined sound of their throaty engines. Everyone looks on in amazement as row upon row of customised Italian Lambrettas and Vespas pass through the high street carrying scores of parka-wearing mods on their journey to the South Coast for the big 'secretive', but well-publicised, bank holiday punch-up with their arch-enemies, the rockers. They casually weave their way through the slow-moving traffic, forcing some car drivers to brake sharply or stop altogether to avoid collisions. The scooter-riding mods soon disappear from view leaving scores of Cortinas, Zephyrs, Minis, Rovers and 1100s stranded in their wake. Young children kneel on car seats and poke their heads out of windows to get a better view. There are no child locks on the car doors; nor are there any special child seats. Kids just jump around in the back of cars, moving from window to window, without any restraints. The cars aren't even fitted with seat belts (how did we manage to survive?). There is only a short gap in the traffic before another group of mods begin to swarm through

the high street on their chrome accessory-laden scooters. Each scooter is fitted with as many chrome fog lamps and mirrors as possible, with chrome crash bars and luggage racks, and reflective chrome bumpers and side panels. The scooter-riding mods are all wearing similar casual clothes underneath their parka jackets: blue Levi jeans, brushed-suede Hush Puppies or desert boots, Fred Perry polo shirts and dark sunglasses. Some distinguish themselves by having their names printed on the small windscreen at the front of their scooters. They're not wearing any crash helmets of course, because that would not suit the cool mod image they seek to portray (it didn't become compulsory to wear crash helmets in the UK until 1973). The queuing young-sters are completely mesmerised by the unusual sight of so many mods on scooters and many fail to even notice when the cinema doors are thrown open for their much-loved Saturday Morning Pictures to begin.

Later that morning, the cinema's exit door slams open to release hundreds of kids back onto the street, some riding on imaginary horses and shooting at passers-by with their outstretched fingers in typical Lone Ranger style. Most of the kids are squinting their eyes to shield them from the sudden shock of daylight. A few of them congregate outside the cinema while they consider what to do next, but most head off in different directions towards their home turfs. One young girl stops outside the Home and Colonial store to peer through the window and watch a man behind the counter slice some bacon on the big slicing machine. She is fascinated by the mechanics of it, as each rotation of the handle produces one evenly sliced piece of bacon, which then falls into a neat pile on some

greaseproof paper. Having satisfied her curiosity with bacon slicing, she walks on a bit further, slowing down to absorb the mixed aroma of fine foods that hang around the shop's main entrance, before stopping again at the next window to observe a lady shop assistant wielding a large cheese wire to slice through an enormous wedge of Cheddar cheese. The young girl presses her nose up against the shop window to get a better view. Her eyes flit from counter to counter as she marvels at all of the appetising foodstuffs they sell and she ponders: 'Could this be the job for me when I leave school?'

A bit further down the high street, some girls have stopped to look at the latest list of top twenty records that has been posted in the window of the Harlequin Records shop. They all scream with delight to see that their current favourite record, *Juliet* by The Four Pennies, has reached number one in the pop charts. Meanwhile, the mischievous boys in their group have nipped into the entrance lobby of John Collier's menswear shop next door to perform an impromptu rendition of the John Collier television jingle: 'John Collier, John Collier – The window to watch!' But their jovial mood soon turns sour when the girls tell them that Chuck Berry's latest record, *No Particular Place To Go*, hasn't yet made it onto the top ten list.

The whole gang have pocket money that is burning holes in their pockets, but none can stretch to the price of a pop record; a seven-inch vinyl single with an A and a B side costs 6s 8d (33.5p in today's money), a seven-inch vinyl EP (extended play) with two or three tunes on each side costs 11s 6d (57.5p) and a twelve-inch vinyl LP (long player) with about six tunes on each side costs £1 12s 3d

(£1.61p). By now, they are all feeling a bit peckish and want something to eat, but they can't agree on what. They decide to split up and meet again later in the park for a game of British Bulldog. The boys head off down the road, past the old 'fleapit' cinema (every town seemed to have a fleapit cinema), towards the market where they are at first tempted by appetising smells coming from the apple fritter stall, but they resist that temptation and continue on past several more market stalls to the next corner where they separate; two walk across the road to Manze's pie and mash shop, while the others join the queue for ice cream sodas at the hatch window of the Italian ice cream parlour. Meanwhile, back on the high street, the girls have already been into Woolworths and cleared much of the stock from the pick 'n' mix counter, and they are now on their way down to the Wavy Line grocer's shop to empty their fridge of four-penny frozen Jubblies.

The Changing Street Scene

At the time, the main streets were still considered to be safe places for kids to roam about unattended. There was plenty of bullying, but you never heard stories of children being mugged for their plimsolls or pocket money, nor did you hear anything about kids being abducted. From a young age kids were told not to talk to strangers and they were taught how to stand up for themselves and how to look after their mates. They seemed to have a built-in instinct for spotting weirdoes and knew that they should keep well away from anyone acting strangely.

It wasn't unusual, especially in big towns and cities, for kids as young as 7 or 8 to go out in the morning with their friends and be missing for hours at a time, sometimes all day. This happened more in the early sixties, when in many areas it was quite normal for people to leave a key hanging down behind the letterbox for children of the house to come and go as they pleased. Everybody knew one another and they were also familiar with all of the regular doorstep tradesmen, like the postman, milkman and breadman, and, of course, 'the man from the Pru'. Everyone seemed to have the Prudential Insurance man call each week to collect small life insurance premiums. The tallyman was often an unwelcome visitor, persistent in persuading people to buy stuff on the never-never that they didn't really need, but equally unrelenting when collecting the unaffordable weekly payments.

Most people felt comfortable with the comings and goings in their local streets and believed themselves to be reasonably safe in their own environment. However, as the years went by, growing numbers of motor vehicles were causing more and more traffic congestion on the main roads, resulting in the greater use of side roads as shortcuts, or rat-runs as they were commonly called. By the midsixties, previously quiet, traffic-free residential streets were becoming congested with large numbers of vehicles passing through, and cars and vans competed for roadside parking spaces outside houses. The popularity of motor-scooters and motorbikes with the mods and rockers only added to the noise and traffic danger, with side roads being turned into unofficial race tracks for their enjoyment. This created a lot more air pollution and noise, and where once small

boys floated their toy boats in rain-filled gullies next to the kerb, there now sat oil-leaking hefty lumps of painted metal. Having your own motorcar was just great, but the ever-increasing use of motor vehicles had damaged the established way of life in local neighbourhoods. People stayed indoors more, and kids were finding that they could no longer play safely in their local streets. Instead, they had to play in each other's back gardens or go to the park to play their games and to find adventure. The days of using jumpers for goalposts in the middle of the street were slowly disappearing and, sadly, the long-established neighbourly community spirit was beginning to wane. Gradually, people were becoming less trusting, more cautious and security conscious. By the end of the sixties we all had our windows and doors securely shut, locked and bolted, day and night. But, thankfully, the days of an Orwellian, 'Big Brother', totalitarian society of surveillance was still a long way off, with no CCTV cameras anywhere to be seen.

Playing Out

Television's much-improved children's programmes and early evening pop music shows were very popular and some became essential viewing for children of all ages. This made it easier than it had been in the past for mums to rein in their children for early evening tea. The magnetism that such television programmes had over kids was such that they would actually keep track of time so as not to miss the start of a programme. By the mid-sixties it was becoming increasingly rare for kids to disappear in the morning and

not come back until after dark, as they often did on non-school days in the past, but most kids still preferred to play outside with their mates and they would take every opportunity to do so, just as long as it didn't interfere with them seeing their favourite television programmes.

There were lots more toys and games available in the 1960s than ever before. Young boys were ditching their Davy Crockett fur hats and Roy Rogers' silver six-shooter cap-guns in favour of the very latest sparking space guns, while girls were proudly dressing, grooming and accessorising their new best friend, the Sindy fashion doll. And, much to the surprise of older kids and grown-ups, young boys were being persuaded by television advertising to put down their tin soldiers and instead play with their very own dolls, in the form of action-hero figures like Action Man, Tommy Gunn and Captain Scarlet. Fortunately, as had always been the case, most of the best outdoor games and adventures could be played without the need for any manufactured toys. The outdoor rough-and-tumble activities and chase games were taught and handed down to you by the older kids, and you learned how to modify them and to make up new games as you went along. Because they played outside all the time, kids became streetwise – again, learning from the older kids. You got up to mischief, but there always seemed to be a policeman, park keeper or warden round every corner to keep you in check. These were the days when a child could expect a clip around the ear if they were caught misbehaving. Policemen were respected and feared; you might give them a bit of cheek, but it would always be from a safe distance. They were all on foot or bicycle back then, so kids, being fit and full of energy, could easily run

away from them. If you did get caught and given a ticking-off by someone in authority then you wouldn't dare go home and tell your dad – there was the fear of being in even more trouble for having been up to mischief in the first place, and woe betide you if you got into any trouble with the police.

Spring and summer were great because of the mild weather, long days and light evenings. A single day could encompass a great number of activities. Nothing was planned for; what you did was dependent upon who was around. If you lived in an ordinary street then the local streets, parks and back gardens were your playgrounds. New high-rise blocks of flats and office blocks were springing up everywhere like uncontrolled weeds. Mostly, they were giant ugly boxes that were constructed using prefabricated concrete cladding and loads of glass. The initial joy of moving from a damp, dilapidated terraced house into one of these modern flats was often short-lived, with many residents having to contend with water ingression, condensation and noise from the neighbouring flats and walkways. The council estates had designated play areas for children, but these were often spoilt by the presence of unruly teenagers, and so again the younger kids often ended up on the streets or in the park. In the early sixties, when it was still considered safe to play in the streets, kids would join in with the games others were playing as and when they came out to play. Skipping, ball games, hopscotch and variations of run-outs were the favourites, and there were lots of pretend games played by the younger kids. Then there were all the doorstep games, like lolly sticks, five stones, jacks and marbles. All of the popular board games were also

played outside, on doorsteps or in front gardens; games like draughts, snakes and ladders, Monopoly, Cluedo, Scrabble, dominoes, Mouse Trap and Ludo. And there were loads of card games, often played using things like lolly sticks, stones or marbles for stakes instead of money.

Bicycles had always been a popular means of transport for people to get to and from work and school, but there seemed to be a lot more of them being used solely for enjoyment in the 1960s. There were lots of small-wheel kids' bikes and shopping bikes, like the Moulton with front and rear carriers for baskets and bags. In 1965 the cheapest Moulton was £24 19s 6d, and the most expensive deluxe model was £31 19s 6d. There were also plenty of traditional straight handlebar Wayfarer-style bikes that cost about £18–£20, but the most sought after were the drop handlebar racing-style bikes, like the Triumph Sportsmaster and the Raleigh Rapide, which cost £18–£31, depending on the size and number of gears. It became more common for kids to go bike riding in groups and to have races and show off by doing wheelies and other tricks on their bikes. Bicycles began to routinely appear on children's Christmas wish-lists as kids' expectations of Christmas presents went up in the freer-spending decade. Whether you had a bicycle or not, there was always the desire to have 'wheels' and everyone enjoyed playing on homemade wooden go-karts, made out of old crates, blocks of wood and discarded pram wheels. You fixed an upright stick to the side, which you pulled back to scrape against the wheel and act as a brake, and there was a piece of rope tied to the front axle for steering. In winter, if you had snow, you would turn your hand to making wooden sledges and head for the nearest hill.

There have always been young 'anoraks' around and it was no different in the 1960s; you could see them at holiday time and weekends standing by the side of the road collecting car registration numbers or trainspotting at draughty railway stations. They always looked pasty-faced and cold, clutching their notebooks and pencils with numb fingertips poking through fingerless woollen gloves, and their trusty fish paste sandwiches and flask always by their side.

Shopping

Britain was renowned as being a nation of shopkeepers and our high streets were full of them. There were very few boarded-up shop fronts and no charity shops; instead, high streets were thriving with retail businesses selling tangible goods. There were, of course, no computer, DVD, video game or mobile phone shops in those days, and DIY superstores were still a few years away. There were very few restaurants, takeaway food shops, travel agents, health shops and licensed betting shops on the average high street. In between the butchers, bakers, florists and newsagents there were all the big name retailers, like Boots, Fine Fare, MacFisheries, Marks & Spencer, Sainsbury's, Tesco, Victor Value, Timothy Whites and Woolworths. Television sets were quite expensive to buy and they weren't very reliable, so it was popular practice for people to rent televisions rather than buy them. Therefore, the high streets were full of competing television rental companies, like DER, Rediffision, and Radio Rentals. There were also lots of specialist shops, like ironmonger, handyman and hobbies shops, with most

high streets having at least one shop selling knitting wool. It was quite common for girls and women to make some of their own clothes and so there were a lot of shops around to supply their sewing needs, with Singer Sewing Machine shops being a familiar sight in many high streets. And, with so many smokers around, there were tobacconist shops and kiosks everywhere, with recognisable names like Finlay. Many of the shop names that were so familiar to us all in the 1960s have, for one reason or another, long since disappeared from our high streets. Some of these have already been mentioned, but there were many others, like Broadmead Radio, Laskys, Chelsea Girl, Cyril Lord Carpets, Times Furnishing, Willoughby Tailoring, Hepworth's Tailors and the Green Shield Stamp catalogue shops. There are hundreds of such names that sadly no longer adorn our high streets, but not all of the missing names belong to retail shops. After all, at one time or another, your mum probably took you to one of the Lyons Tea Shops for afternoon tea, or, if you lived in London, you might have even been treated to something a bit classier at one of the art deco-style Lyons Corner Houses. You probably had your first grown-up meal out in a Berni Inn, with prawn cocktail to start and Black Forest gateau to finish – very sophisticated! Or perhaps you just drooled over a scrumptious Brown Derby at the local Wimpy bar.

There were some small arcades around, mostly with little open-fronted lock-up shops and kiosks, but nothing anywhere near as grand as the shopping malls we have today. People did all of their shopping in the high street shops and from stalls in street markets. There was very little covered shopping and so topcoats and umbrellas were a must

This mid-sixties Tesco advertisement shows cut prices being offered on a range of food products. The Green Shield Stamps sign was added to Tesco advertisements in 1964, which was the year they first started to offer these stamps on customer purchases.

in the winter. Sometimes, in the big street markets there would be 'Del Boy' characters literally selling things off the back of a lorry. All sorts of stuff for the home: electric blankets, sheets, towels, cutlery and, the favourite, crockery. The front man, who always had the gift of the gab, would stand on the rear section of the lorry trailer spouting his sales pitch at full volume so as to pull in as many punters as possible. From a few feet away, his assistant would chuck plates for him to catch one at a time to build up an unbelievable bargain offer. 'Here you are ladies, one, two, three, four, five, six dinner plates.' Then, one at a time, his assistant throws him six small side plates, which he adds to the pile of dinner plates already in his hand, and fans the lot out to display them to the assembled crowd. 'There you are ladies!' (it was always a crowd of ladies). 'Six dinner plates, and six side plates, all the best bone china. And, hang on a minute, I'll throw in a set of six matching cereal bowls.' Again, his assistant throws him six cereal bowls, one at a time, which he catches and adds to the front of the fanned-out display of crockery. 'There you go ladies, a bone china dinner service like this would set you back £20 on the high street, but I'm not going to ask you to pay £20, I'm not even going to ask you to pay £15, or even £10. No, hang on a minute, today I feel generous and I'm going to chuck in six matching cups and saucers, and I'm still not going to charge you £10. Not £10, not even £8! No ladies, today I'm going to let you have this thirty-piece set of best bone china at a give-away price of just £7 for the lot.' By now there are many outstretched hands waving money in the air, with lots of punters desperate to get a set. 'Take the ladies' money', are the front man's parting words

as he moves away, and four of his previously unseen helpers appear from the shadows, laden with factory-packed boxed sets of the crockery. 'No, we don't take cheques lady. If we wanted to take cheques then we would have opened a bank account and told the tax man.' Throughout the sale, the front man regularly hints that the consignment is not legal and has fallen off the back of a lorry, but the police were always watching from a distance and the more likely scenario was that these traders dealt in bankrupt stock, which they bought for next to nothing at auction. 'Come on ladies, I've only got six left, who's having them? When they're gone, they're gone!' The final six are snapped up in seconds and 'Del Boy' and his helpers start to present another bargain offer to the assembled crowd. This time it's a set of top-quality cotton towels.

I wonder how many mums struggled home on the bus, weighted down with their unwieldy box of crockery, musing over why they had bought it when they didn't really need it, and where they were going to put it when they got it home? But it was a bargain!

The street markets were fascinating places for kids to wander around. All the wheeling and dealing of market traders and lots of joking around, with all the stallholders smoking half-chewed roll-up cigarettes and drinking endless mugs of tea held by cold fingers. It was a real education, but a frightening prospect for any child considering what they will do for a living when they leave school – probably best to find a job in a nice warm cosy office somewhere.

Pocket Money

You weren't doing too badly if you got a half crown for pocket money each week to spend on whatever you wanted. Some kids didn't get a fixed amount of pocket money, but instead got spoon-fed money during the week for sweets, comics and other treats. It was always best to get a fixed amount of pocket money on a Saturday and then try for extras during the week. The only problem with getting a fixed amount was that you were always under pressure to save some in your piggy bank or to buy post office savings stamps. It did teach you the value of money and how to manage it – when it was gone, it was gone. Mind you, a half crown didn't go very far in the mid-sixties. The *Beano* and *Dandy* comics were still only 3*d* each, but some of the girls' magazines, like *Boyfriend* and *June*, were 7*d* each, and boys' magazines like *Meccano* cost 1*s* 6*d*. If you wanted to keep up with all the latest news and pictures of The Beatles then the monthly Beatles book was also 1*s* 6*d*, and the weekly *New Musical Express* was 5*d*. By the time you paid to get into Saturday Morning Pictures and bought a few sweets and a Jubbly, there wasn't much left. Pre-teenage kids of the 1960s were often as keen on music and fashions as the older teenagers were, but their involvement was limited by the amount of pocket money they got. Many relied on older siblings to buy the latest pop records, and that was okay if you had similar tastes in music, but it could be a nightmare if you were opposites. A young boy fan of the Rolling Stones' music didn't really want to hear Billy Fury's soppy love songs bellowing out from his big sister's bedroom. If you were lucky, you might get the odd hand-me-down piece

of trendy clothing to wear. For boys, a well-worn and faded pair of blue Levi jeans was always a welcome cast-off from a big brother, while girls delighted in anything that a big sister might give to them. Of course, there were the inevitable rows between siblings over unauthorised borrowing of clothes and accessories, mostly between sisters.

Although there were age restrictions and rules regarding employing children, there was much less bureaucracy than there is now, and many young kids earned extra pocket money by doing some form of paid casual work. Early morning newspaper rounds were popular, as was car washing and helping the milkman; the local milkmen all seemed to have young helpers travelling with them on their milk floats, helping to sort out the orders and carry bottles of milk to customers' doorsteps. It was mostly unofficial and poorly paid work, but kids would grab at the chance to earn an extra few bob for their pocket money. Lifting boxes down at the market, restocking shop shelves, collecting newspapers and rags, running errands, babysitting, returning beer and lemonade bottles to the off-licence to get back the thruppence a bottle deposit. There was always some way of boosting your pocket money.

To manage your pocket money, you first needed to learn the complicated calculations of pounds, shillings and pence, which most kids picked up quickly from a very young age. The coins and notes that we all used in the 1960s have been referred to as 'old money' since decimalisation took place in 1971. The 'old money' was written down using the L.S.D. symbols £ s d, which were abbreviations for 'pounds, shillings and pence'. The '£' symbol was used for the pound and comes from the Latin word *librum* (a Roman unit of weight

derived from the Latin word for 'scales'). The '*s*' symbol was used for the shilling and comes from the Latin word *solidus* (a Roman gold coin derived from the Latin word for 'whole'). The '*d*' symbol was used for pence and comes from the Latin word *denarius* (a common Roman coin). There were some peculiarities about the way we used and spoke about money. Sometimes expensive items would be sold in units of 1 guinea, which was equal to 21*s*, but the coin itself no longer existed in the 1960s; in fact, the guinea coin had not been struck since 1799. Money was often referred to by slang names such as brass, dosh, dough, folding stuff, lolly, moola or readies. A group of farthings, halfpennies and pennies was called 'coppers', meaning a small amount of money, as in 'just a few coppers'. Something costing 'one and a half pennies' would be called 'threehaypence' or 'threehaypenny worth', as in 'three halfpennies'. It was quite normal for a shop to only use shillings and pence when pricing low-value goods, so a pair of shoes might be advertised at 49/11*d* rather than £2 9*s* 11*d*. There was no two-pence coin, but everyone regularly used the words 'tuppence' or 'tuppenny'. Money would sometimes be used to describe people, as in the term 'not quite the full shilling'.

Here is a list of the main pre-decimalisation coins and notes with the old English slang words sometimes used to refer to them:

> Farthing (¼*d*) (4 farthings = 1 old penny).
>
> Halfpenny (½*d*) Usually pronounced 'Hay-p-nee'.
>
> Penny (1*d*) (12 pennies = 1 shilling).
>
> Three pence (3*d*) Usually pronounced 'thruppence' or a 'thruppenny-bit', and the old silver threepence was called a 'joey'.

Six pence (6*d*) Also known as a 'tanner' or a 'kick'.

Shilling (1/-) Also known as a 'bob' or a 'shilling-bit'. (20 shillings = 1 pound).

Two shillings (2/-) Also known as a 'florin' or a 'two-bob-bit'. (10 florins = 1 pound).

Half crown (2/6) Also known as 'half-a-dollar' or 'two-and-a-kick'. (1 half crown = 2 shillings and six old pence).

Crown (5/-) (rarely found in circulation) Sometimes called a 'dollar'. (1 crown = 5 shillings).

Ten-shilling note (10/-) Also known as a 'ten-bob-note', 'half-a-nicker' or 'half-a-bar'.

One pound note (£1) Also known as a 'quid', 'nicker', or a 'bar'.

Sweets and Treats

The pick 'n' mix counter in Woolworths was always a joy for kids, with all of that variety and no shopkeeper to moan about having to open lots of different jars when you asked for a quarter of a pound of mixed sweets; mind you, there was something special about going into an old dusty sweetshop with high wooden counters jam-packed with boxes of penny-chews and other sweet delights to tease the pennies out of your pocket. Lucky bags, Sherbet dips, Wagon Wheels, blackjacks, fruit salads, liquorice sticks and pipes, gobstoppers, sherbet lemons, Rowntree's fruit gums and fruit pastilles, Spangles, chocolate coins in gold foil wrappers, sherbet flying saucers, Bubblegum, Fruitellas, Catherine Wheels, Love Hearts, Refreshers, Shrimps, Sherbet Fountains, Walnut Whips and Barrett's sweet cigarettes with football cards. Behind the counter, the shelves

A 1960 magazine advertisement for the popular mint-flavoured Spangles with the pink stripe.

along the wall were chock-a-block with huge jars of sweets that you bought by weight, usually in 2 ounces or quarter pound (4 ounce) measures. There were hundreds of different sweets: pear drops, aniseed balls, Kola Kubes, sweet peanuts, sugar almonds, nut brittle, fruit bonbons, sherbet lemons, milk gums, jelly babies, jelly beans, dolly mixtures, American Hard Gums, Liquorice Allsorts, chocolate honeycomb, marshmallows, and loads more. Remember those small, narrow 2*d* packets of KP nuts and the Smith's potato crisps bags with the blue twist wrapper of salt that always found its way to the very bottom of the bag, making you rummage through all of the crisps to find it. In 1962, at long last, Golden Wonder introduced cheese and onion flavoured crisps. How did we manage to exist before there were cheese and onion flavoured crisps?

On hot summer days it was hard to resist the taste of a Lyons' Mivvi or a Wall's Split ice cream on a stick, coated with a shell of strawberry-flavoured ice. But, when it was really hot, there was nothing more satisfying than a frozen Jubbly, which was frozen orange juice in an unusual triangular-shaped carton. You would tear one corner of the carton and suck the frozen orange juice like an ice-lolly, but without a lollystick. As you held it in your warm hands, the orange juice would start to melt into the bottom of the carton, which allowed you to turn it up and drink the juice through the hole in the top corner. It took ages to finish a Jubbly, much longer than any of the fancy shaped ice-lolly alternatives, like Zoom, Orbit, Fab and Sea Jet.

It wasn't just sweets and ices that were popular in sweetshops. Scoubidous were all the rage and the coloured plastic strips needed to make them were displayed on the

sweetshop counters. Scoubidous were fun to make and they would keep you occupied for hours. You would plait the plastic strips together to make all sorts of colourful things, like bracelets and animal figures. Some kids made long colourful plaits to hang from their bicycle handlebars, but the easiest and most useful thing that everyone made was a Scoubidou key ring. Outside the sweetshops, the bubble gumball vending machines were always a big temptation for the younger kids. The machines were often chained to the outside wall of sweetshops; sometimes there were two machines, with one containing cheap and nasty plastic toys.

Bonfire Night

The nights started to draw in very quickly once the summer holidays were over and everyone was back at school; all of a sudden it was autumn and all the fun of playing outside ground to a halt. All those miserable dark evenings and little to look forward to until Christmas, which was still many weeks away. There was just one event that broke the monotony of being stuck indoors watching television on dark, damp, autumn nights, and that was Bonfire Night on the fifth of November. Many kids started planning for Bonfire Night well in advance; collecting and storing wood and other flammable materials as far back as September. The task of earning money to buy fireworks would start a couple of weeks before the big event, towards the end of October. It basically involved begging for money on street corners in aid of a home-

This 1960 advertisement for Standard Fireworks captures a typical schoolboy's excitement on Bonfire Night.

made effigy of Guy Fawkes that you had stuffed with newspapers and dressed in old clothes, with a football for a head and a paper facemask. The begging cry was, 'Penny for the Guy!' but you always expected more.

Restrictions on the sale of fireworks were not as tight as they are today and so kids could buy fireworks and matches fairly easily. But any fireworks that were bought before Guy Fawkes Night had to be used straight away, as most mums wouldn't allow them to be stored inside the house; not with all those open fires and lit cigarettes. For boys, the objective was to get as many bangs as possible for their money, and so most of their firework money was spent on penny bangers. The fancy fireworks, like Roman candles and rockets, were expensive and could be unreliable and therefore a waste of money, not to mention dangerous. On the night itself, once the last few pieces of timber had been put in place and the 'Guy' was suitably fixed on top of the wood mountain, the bonfire was lit. Everyone would stand back to watch as the fire took hold and the bonfire began to blaze, and then all hell broke loose. Bonfire Night always seemed to bring out the evil in boys, who had more fun frightening the girls than watching the colourful displays of exploding rockets in the night sky. Bonfire Night was both exciting and dangerous. You never knew when a penny banger was going to fly past your nose. Girls ducked their heads and screamed in fear as bottles that were supposed to be supporting upright rocket launches fell over and sent rockets whizzing across open ground. While people covered their heads to shelter from the debris of spent rockets falling from the sky, mischievous and menacing boys threw Catherine wheels and jumping crackers along the ground, just for the joy of scaring the life

out of everyone. The lead up to Bonfire Night was often more exciting than the night itself. The eye-catching bonfires and firework displays were somewhat overshadowed by the dirty smoke-filled air and the horrible stench of sulphur. Fireworks' Night was never complete without the familiar sound of fire engine and ambulance bells. It was always a dangerous night to be out and every year a lot of people got injured. Can't wait for next year!

Remember, remember, the fifth of November,
The Gunpowder, Treason and Plot,
I can think of no reason
Why the Gunpowder Treason
Should ever be forgot.

Buying a bike? See the special section inside

meccano
magazine

November
1s.6d.

the practical boy's hobbies magazine

IN THIS ISSUE

Build a transistor radio

Plans for a control line model aircraft

1964

Four

GAMES, HOBBIES
AND PASTIMES

Lots of new toys and board games were launched in the
1960s and kids had far more things to play with than ever
before. There was also the benefit of having television in the
home, which many less fortunate 1950s kids had missed out
on. There was a choice of two television channels to watch
– ITV or BBC – and from 1964, if you had one of the latest
625-line television sets, then you could even pick up the
new BBC2 channel. But having three television channels
to choose from meant that you were more likely to wear
a hole in the carpet, going backwards and forwards from
the sofa to the television set to manually change channels.
There were none of the technological trappings that are

now part of everyday life, but you didn't feel lacking in any way. On the contrary, you were too busy enjoying the progressive sixties to even consider that there could be much better things to come in the future. After all, you could now get stereo record players, transistor radios, felt-tip pens, electric blankets, digital clocks, Velcro, Lego, audio cassette and 8-track tape recorders, and Teasmade automatic tea-making machines – and we even had men landing on the moon. It was all very new and exciting stuff, and to top it all there was the great new board game, Mousetrap. Okay, so you didn't have computers, mobile phones, games consoles, MP3 and video players, digital cameras, Sky TV, CDs and DVDs, and you didn't even have pocket calculators. Astonishingly, most people managed to get right to the end of the sixties without upgrading to a colour television set. In hindsight, it is amazing to think that everyone managed to live quite happily without any of these things and kids never seemed to have any problem keeping themselves occupied.

Even on cold and wet days, when you were reluctantly stuck indoors, there was always something to do. Most kids had some sort of hobby to keep them busy and there were lots of board and card games to play. There were plenty of books, magazines and comics to read, and crossword puzzles to do. You made stuff out of beads, cloth and wood, and tried your hand at making objects out of papier mâché. You messed around with Play-Doh and Plasticine and made Airfix and Meccano models. Well, the boys did. That is if they weren't too busy playing with their electric train set or their much-cherished Scalextric car racing game.

Hidden away somewhere in your bedroom, you will surely have had your very own secret box of treasures where

Play-Doh modelling compound was developed and marketed in the US during the late 1950s, but we had to wait until 1964 for it to be sold in Britain's toy shops. This advertisement appeared in British magazines in November 1964.

you kept all of your most valued possessions. To anyone else it was a load of junk, but each and every object was special to you: a Beatles' lapel badge, a broken watch with no strap, a dented metal thimble, a leaky fountain pen, some copper coins, a couple of marbles and a small piece of chalk. There were always a couple of strange, obscure items in there, like a Watneys Red Barrel beer mat or one of your dad's old cigarette lighters. I suppose it was a load of old rubbish, but everyone liked to collect things: stamps, postcards, marbles, cigarette cards, Dinky toys, coins, badges, gonk and troll dolls. And, of course, you will have collected sack loads of aluminium foil milk bottle tops and sent them off to *Blue Peter* for them to raise money to buy guide dogs for the blind.

Beatles merchandise was plentiful in the 1960s, and this advertisement for an official embroidered sew-on badge appeared in *The Beatles Book* (monthly edition No 9) in April 1964.

From a young age, girls were taught how to sew and knit, and many were keen to use those skills to make things for themselves. Often starting with something simple like a stuffed animal toy or a new outfit for their doll, then progressing on to the serious stuff of making fashionable clothes for themselves. Even 'baby boomer' and fashion icon Twiggy used to make her own clothes when she was a young girl, before she was famous. A lot of girls were eager to learn and develop other skills as well, like embroidery, cooking and baking, and they practised them whenever they could. Children's bedrooms were just furnished with the basics, they didn't have their own television or computer and so there was no reason for them to shut themselves away from the rest of the family for hours at a time. Instead, girls spent a great deal of time with their mums, and it was the norm for mothers to teach their daughters all the things that were then regarded as feminine skills, just as their mums had taught them when they were young girls.

The quality and choice of radio and television programmes improved a lot during the sixties and so we did listen to more radio and watch an increasing amount of television, but often while doing something else at the same time. Simple indoor hobbies like stamp collecting and scrap-booking were still popular, but our favourite times were spent outdoors playing games and exploring. Boys armed themselves with their catapults, peashooters, space-guns and water balloons; and girls dressed up in their mum's frock and high heels, trailing a skipping rope behind them. From homemade kites to wooden go-karts, we had everything we needed to have fun. And then there were all the cost-free street games we played. There were hundreds of

them, many handed down through the generations, and we played them all. There were lots of different variations of the same game being played around the country, but they were basically the same. Here are a few to jog the memory and remind you of all those times that you crossed your fingers and shouted 'fainites!' But first you need to decide who is going to be 'it'.

Boatman Boatman, Farmer Farmer (young kids' version of British Bulldogs): One person was chosen to be 'it' and became the boatman. The boatman stood in the middle of a pre-agreed play area and all the other players stood on a line at one edge. The players then chanted, 'Boatman, Boatman, can we cross the river?' The boatman replied, 'You can only cross the river if you are wearing (name of a colour).' Any player wearing something of that colour then crossed freely to the other side of the play area. The players that were not wearing the required colour had to run to the other side without being caught by the boatman. Any players that were caught then joined the boatman as catchers, and the game was repeated until there was only one uncaught player left and he or she was the winner.

British Bulldogs, Bulldog, Bullies, Red Rover, Runno: Any number of boys and girls would join in to play this, but it was not for the faint-hearted; this game would usually result in a few injuries, particularly when played on a hard surface or if played by mixed age groups. The favoured places to play this were in fields and on bomb ruin sites. To start with, one or two players were selected to be bulldogs and they were made to stand in the middle of the field. There were two safe areas on opposite side edges of the field. All of the non-bulldogs gathered in one of these safe

areas. The main objective of the game was for the non-bull-dogs to run across the field from one safe area to the other without being caught by the bulldogs. The game started with one of the bulldogs naming a player that was to be the first to attempt the run from one side to the other, and the bulldogs would then attempt to catch the runner. If he or she was caught by a bulldog then the bulldog had to hold onto the failed runner and shout 'British Bulldog; one, two, three!' The caught runner then became a bulldog. If he or she did reach the other side without being caught then they were deemed to be in the safe area and could not be caught. Once the runner had either been caught or reached the safe area then all the other non-bulldogs had to immediately attempt to cross the playing area themselves (this was called the 'rush' or 'bullrush'), with the bulldogs trying to catch as many as possible using the same rules as before. Once all the surviving non-bulldogs had reached the 'safe' area on the other side of the field, the rush began again to get across the field in the opposite direction, avoiding the bulldogs. The game continued until all the players had become bull-dogs, and the winner was the last person to be caught. It was quite difficult to catch someone and hold on to them for enough time to shout 'British Bulldog; one, two, three!' It usually needed some tough rugby tackling, which resulted in grubby and torn clothes and countless bruises, cuts and grazes. As with other games, various versions were played around the country with other local names being used to describe it.

Cat's Cradle: A game for two people, usually girls, to create a series of patterns, including the 'cat's cradle', out of a loop of string wrapped around the fingers and wrists.

Individual girls, sometimes with the use of their teeth, created simpler creations, like a 'cup and saucer'.

Conkers: The game was played by two children, each with a conker threaded onto a piece of string or an old shoelace. One player would let the conker dangle on the full length of the string while the other player swung their conker to hit it. The players took turns to strike each other's conker until one broke. Sometimes it was the attacking conker that broke. The conkers were given names to identify their worth; a new conker was called a 'none-er', and when a 'none-er' broke another 'none-er' it became a 'one-er', then a 'two-er', 'three-er', and so on. The winning conker inherited the previous score of the losing conker as well as gaining the score from that particular game. So if a 'two-er' beat a 'three-er' then the winning conker became a 'six-er'. The hardest conkers usually won, but there was a lot of cheating, with players using various methods to aid the hardening of their conkers, including soaking them in vinegar overnight, baking them in the oven for a short time and seasoning them by keeping them for a year before use.

Egg, Egga, Bad Egg (played with a tennis ball): The person who was 'it' would give the players a subject like colours or football teams to choose a name from. The players would huddle together to whisper and choose names. One of the players would then call out loud all of the names chosen by the players. The person who was 'it' would then throw the ball high into the air or against a wall and shout out one of the names (i.e. blue or Arsenal), and the player that had chosen that name would have to catch or retrieve the ball while the others ran away. Once the person had retrieved the ball, he or she would shout 'Stop!' or 'Egg!', or

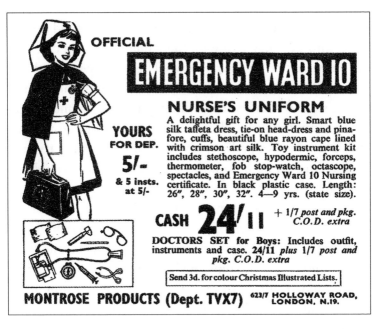

OFFICIAL

EMERGENCY WARD 10

NURSE'S UNIFORM

A delightful gift for any girl. Smart blue silk taffeta dress, tie-on head-dress and pinafore, cuffs, beautiful blue rayon cape lined with crimson art silk. Toy instrument kit includes stethoscope, hypodermic, forceps, thermometer, fob stop-watch, octascope, spectacles, and Emergency Ward 10 Nursing certificate. In black plastic case. Length: 26″, 28″, 30″, 32″. 4—9 yrs. (state size).

YOURS FOR DEP.

5/-

& 5 insts. at 5/-

CASH 24/11 + 1/7 *post and pkg. C.O.D. extra*

DOCTORS SET for Boys: Includes outfit, instruments and case. 24/11 *plus* 1/7 *post and pkg. C.O.D. extra*

Send 3d. for colour Christmas Illustrated Lists.

MONTROSE PRODUCTS (Dept. TVX7) 623/7 **HOLLOWAY ROAD, LONDON, N.19.**

This nurse's uniform for young girls was typical of the merchandise that was sold following the success of Britain's first hospital-based television drama series, *Emergency Ward 10*. It was advertised during the period leading up to Christmas 1962.

something similar, and the players would have to stand still. The person with the ball could then take up to three giant steps towards any of the scattered players, and throw the ball at that person. If the ball hit the target then he or she would become 'it' and a new game would begin. If the thrower missed then he or she would be 'it'.

Five Stones (known to me as 'Gobs'): This game was often played on doorsteps and involved five evenly sized small stones and one larger stone, with the player using just one hand. One person would play at a time by placing one

of the small stones on the back of his or her hand and throwing it into the air, picking up the larger stone and catching the thrown stone on its way down. This was repeated, adding one small stone to the back of the hand at each throw until all five small stones had been thrown into the air and caught at the same time as picking up the large stone. Your turn ended if you dropped any of the stones or failed to pick up the large stone before the small stones were caught in the palm of your hand. In an alternative version, you would throw the five small stones onto the ground and place the large stone on the back of your hand. You would then throw the large stone in the air and pick up one small stone from the ground before catching the large stone on its way down. You would continue to pick up one stone at a time until you had all five small stones and the one large stone in the palm of your hand. This was called 'onesies'. If you were successful then you would start again with five small stones on the ground, but this time pick up to two small stones at a time (called 'twosies'). If you continued to be successful then you would then progress to 'threesies', 'foursies' and 'fivesies'. You were allowed to throw the large stone up from the back of your hand and sweep the small stones on the ground together with your fingers, but if you used this tactic then you had to catch the large stone on the back of your hand in between each sweep.

French Skipping (also known as Elastics): This was a girl's game, played using a very long piece of knicker elastic tied into a loop. Two or more girls would stand inside the loop of elastic, a few feet apart, with the elastic stretched around the outside of their ankles. The first player would then perform a series of skipping movements on, under and over

the elastic. Both feet under the elastic, both feet on top of the elastic, one on top and one under, one on top and one under and then swap feet. The player would then move around one girl to the next section of elastic and repeat the skipping movement. The skips or jumps were often done in time to a skipping rhyme. If the player successfully completed a round of jumps without tripping over or making a mistake, then the elastic would be moved up to knee level (called 'knee-sies'), then thigh level ('thigh-sies'), and then waist level ('waist-sies'). The player would be out if she failed to do the correct jump, and then one of the others would come out from the elastic to have a go.

He, It, Tag, Tig, Tip: Known by various names, this was the simplest and most basic game of chase for a group of kids to play. The person chosen to be 'it' ran around trying to touch or 'tag' one of the others. When touched or tagged then that person became 'it' until he or she touched another player. You could avoid being 'tagged' by lifting your feet off the ground temporarily, by pulling yourself up onto a wall or a bar so that your feet dangled just above the ground. There were loads of optional rules for this game.

He Ball: Similar game to He, It, Tag, Tig and Tip, except with 'He Ball' the person that was 'it' chased the other players with a ball. If 'it' managed to throw the ball and hit a player then that player would become 'it'.

Hopscotch: Usually played in the street. A set of eight or ten equal-sized joined-up squares was chalked onto the pavement in a hopscotch pattern and each square was then numbered. The first player would stand behind the starting line and toss a stone into square number 'one' and then hop over square 'one' and land in square 'two' on one leg,

then continue hopping through the hopscotch, landing on one leg in single squares and two legs in double squares. At the end you would turn around and make your way back down through the hopscotch until you reached the square number 'two'. You would then bend down and pick up the stone from square number 'one', hop into square 'one' and back to the start again. You then threw the stone into square number 'two' and repeated the hopping process as before, only this time hopping over square number 'two' as you made your way through the hopscotch. You repeated this through all the numbered squares, always hopping over the square with the stone in it. A player was deemed to be out if the stone failed to land within the lines of the correct square, he or she stepped into the square where the stone was, put two feet down in a single box, stepped on any of the chalked lines, or lost his or her balance while bending over to pick up the stone. If you managed to complete the whole hopscotch successfully then you hopped through the whole hopscotch again without a stone in any box, and out the top of the hopscotch to finish.

Hula hoop: The hula hoop craze hit Britain in 1958 with the arrival of the American Wham-O toy company's lightweight tubular plastic hoop, made from a recently invented durable plastic, and called the hula hoop. However, the craze was short-lived and only lasted for a few months. But Wham-O relaunched the hula hoop in the late 1960s and it became popular again. The idea was that you twirled the hoop around your waist, limbs or neck for as long as possible, and you had competitions between friends to see who could keep it going for the longest time. It was most popular with the girls, and grown-up women also enjoyed

it as a way to keep fit. Boys were a bit too 'cool' to be seen gyrating their hips to keep a silly hoop in the air.

Jacks: This game was very similar to Five Stones except it was played using a small bouncy rubber ball or a table tennis ball, and between five and ten small stones. You would bounce the ball once and pick up stones, then catch the ball before it bounced again. As with Five Stones, you played 'onesies', 'twosies', 'threesies', 'foursies', 'fivesies', 'sixies' etc., but again, there were several versions to the game.

Knock Down Ginger: A game that was mainly played after dark and could get you into serious trouble with your mum and dad. In its simplest form, you knocked on street doors and ran away without being seen. Most people still had knockers on their street doors in the 1960s. More advanced players would quietly tie cotton to a street door knocker and then reel the cotton out to the other side of the street, where you would hide and then pull the cotton until it broke, thus lifting the knocker and dropping it back in place to create a loud knock on the door. Sometimes you would do three or four knockers at the same time, but that was risky because there was more of a chance that one of the victims might come out and chase after you.

Lolly Sticks: Played with a bunch of used flat wooden lolly sticks. The lolly sticks were held a few inches above the ground and dropped into a heap. You then picked up all of the sticks that weren't touching any of the others and used one of these to move or flick each stick off the pile without moving any of the others. If you moved another stick while flicking then one of the other players started a new game. The winner was the player that had picked up the most sticks during their turn.

Marbles: There were many different versions of Marbles and usually the rules were agreed before the game started. In its simplest form, players took turns to roll or flick marbles at their opponents' marbles and if they hit one then that marble became theirs. Sometimes the game was played within an agreed area or circle, in which case you had to flick your marbles from the edge of the circle without encroaching. The aim was to either hit one of your opponents' marbles that had already been placed near to the centre of the circle at the start of the game, or to knock one of their marbles out of the circle. If you were successful then your 'shooter' marble remained where it had stopped in the circle and you could shoot again from that spot. If you were unsuccessful then the next player began his or her go from outside the circle. Loads of different versions and rules!

Popular children's books from the 1960s.

These Jack and Jill storybook annuals were always popular with young children.

Roller Skating: In the 1960s, children's roller skates were still quite primitive. They were simply four ball-bearing metal wheels attached to a foot-shaped flat piece of metal. You put your foot onto the flat metal plate, with your heel pressed against a small metal ridge at the back. There was a leather strap attached to the back of the skates, which you would wrap around your instep to hold the skates on. At the front, there was an adjustable metal grip on each side, and you tightened these against your shoe to hold the front of your shoe in place. They were absolutely useless! Impossible to keep attached for more than a few minutes at a time. You would often see a lone skate hurtling down the road having escaped the wearer, and sometimes the skate would still have a shoe attached to it. Lots of twisted ankles and grazed knees, but you always went back to have another go!

Run Outs: The person that was 'it' would close his or her eyes and count to an agreed number, usually between ten and one hundred, while the players ran and hid. 'It' would then go in search of the players and each one he or she found would join in to search for the remaining hidden players. The players could change their hiding place during the game as long as they weren't seen by any of the searchers. The last player to be found would be the winner. Seekers would often call out the names of hidden players in the hope that they would answer, and sometimes they did!

Scissors, Paper, Stone: A simple game that was usually played to determine who was to go first in a game, or who was 'it', or who should do a dare. Best played with up to three people, but when played with more than two people there were lots of drawn games, which meant playing again. Being a very fast game, you sometimes played best of three. The players would form a circle and each player would hold out their arm and make a loose fist. You would then shake your fist up and down counting 'one-two-three' and on the downward stroke of 'three' you would open your fist to reveal either 'scissors' – two fingers open, 'paper' – flat open hand, or 'stone' – clenched fist. The winner would be determined as follows:

Scissors cuts paper – scissors wins

Paper wraps stone – paper wins

Stone blunts scissors – stone wins

Skipping (with rope): Very popular, mainly played by girls and usually done in time to a skipping rhyme. A skipping rope, often adapted from mum's washing line, was never

Stamp collecting was a very popular children's hobby, with plenty of letters and postcards dropping through the letterbox in those days, long before email and text messaging existed.

too far away to bring into use when someone suggested it. Girls would often skip alone, but it was best played as a group competition. Depending upon the number of players, the rope would be turned by one girl at either end, or one girl would turn the rope with the other end tied to a lamppost. The turners get the rope to slap the pavement in time to a skipping rhyme being chanted by the skippers. There were loads of rhymes with key words and phrases that prompted the skipper to do a trick in one turn of the rope; like jumping extra high with both feet together, hopping the rope very close to the ground, kicking one foot out, crossing and uncrossing feet and legs, and turning to face the other way. Boys were always fascinated by the skill of the girls and the tricks they could do. The skipper would run out from the turning rope, around one of the girls twirling it, and back in time to the beat of the skipping rope hitting the pavement. Certain phrases in the rhymes would invite other girls to join with, or to take over from, the skipper on the next turn of the rope. Double Dutch was really difficult, with two turning ropes for the skipper to negotiate. There were names for all the tricks, like Kick (kicking one foot out), Sizzler (crossing and uncrossing feet) and Split (opening legs wide apart). There were many skipping variations and so many rhymes, with several different versions adapted around the country.

Georgie Porgie Puddin' Pie
Kissed the girls and made them cry
He kissed them once, then kissed them twice,
How many tears did they cry?

1, 2, 3, 4, 5 …
(Count until someone messes up)

Cinderella dressed in Yellow
Went upstairs to kiss a fellow
Made a mistake and kissed a snake
How many doctors did it take?
1, 2, 3, 4, 5 …
(Count until someone messes up)

I like coffee, I like tea, I want [name] to jump in with me!

Salt, Mustard, Vinegar, Pepper!

Tin Tan Tommy: Played with an old tin can. One person was chosen to be 'it' and a place was designated to be the 'home' point, where the tin can would sit while the game was played. To start the game, one of the players would throw the tin can as hard as he or she could, away from the 'home' point. Whoever was 'it' would chase after the can to retrieve it and return it to 'home'. Meanwhile, all the others would run and hide. Once the can was back in place on the 'home' spot, the person who was 'it' would go and search for the other players. When one was discovered, 'it' would run back to the can and bash it up and down on the ground while shouting 'Tin Tan Tommy, I see Mickey behind the wall', or something similar. But if the discovered person could get back to the can and bash it on the ground before 'it', then he or she was 'home' and safe, otherwise that person became 'it' and another game began.

An advertisement for Meccano, every schoolboy's favourite model
construction kit, appeared in magazines leading up to Christmas 1964.

Two-Balls (juggling with tennis balls): A girls' game that
was usually played by juggling with two balls in the air or
against a wall, but sometimes the girls would use three or
four balls. It was a skill that was mastered by most girls at a
very young age, and although boys admired the skills, they
saw it as a girl's game and usually steered clear of it. Playing
two-balls was always done to the beat of a chanted rhyme.
There were lots of tricks that were described with words
like plainsy, upsy, over, dropsy, bouncy, legsy, twirly. Such
words were inserted in the rhymes to indicate when to
do a certain movement with a ball … One, two, three and
PLAINSY; four, five, six and PLAINSY …

Over the garden wall
I let my baby sister fall;

My mother came out
And gave me a clout,
I told my mother
Not to boss me about;
She gave me another
To match the other,
Over the garden wall.

Juggling two-balls against the pavement was usually done to the rhyme *One Two Three O'Leary*.

Up the Wall: Usually played with cigarette cards or other collecting cards from packets of Barrett's sweets or Brooke Bond Tea cards. Teenagers sometimes played it with coins (farthings, halfpennies and pennies). From an agreed spot, a few feet away from a wall, you would flick your card or coin forwards as accurately as possible. The player who got nearest the wall won and took all the cards or coins already along the ground.

What's the Time Mr Wolf?: One person was chosen to be 'it' and a place was designated to be the 'home' point. The player who was 'it' was called Mr Wolf (sometimes Mr Fox or Mr Bear), and would either stand with his or her back to the other players or be walking slowly away from them. The players would slowly creep up on Mr Wolf chanting, 'What's the time Mr Wolf?' The wolf would stop, turn around and reply, 'It's one o'clock'. The players would continue to ask, 'What's the time Mr Wolf?' and the wolf would reply, 'It's two o'clock', 'three o'clock', until eventually the wolf would reply, 'It's DINNERTIME!' Mr Wolf would then chase the other players who had to return to the 'home' point without being caught. The first person to be caught became Mr Wolf.

Five

MUSIC, FASHION AND CINEMA

As a child of the sixties, you couldn't understand why your mum wouldn't let you choose all of your own clothes or let you have your hair cut like your favourite pop star. You will, at some time or other, have stood in front of the mirror miming to a pop record while using a hairbrush as your microphone. You could never have imagined that the music you grew up with, and so proficiently mimed to all those years ago, would still be played on the radio in the next century, and that many of the 1960s icons that you once raved about would continue to be regularly pictured and reported on in the media for several decades to come. There are particular sounds and images that always fire up personal

memories and remind you of certain times and events from your childhood; lots of these are common to us all and seem to epitomise life as it was back then. Seeing or hearing any of these immediately transports us back in time. Such things include the music of certain pop groups, like the Walker Brothers, anything sung by Donovan, old photographs of Twiggy or 'The Shrimp', the sight of an E-Type Jaguar out on the open road, images of the 1966 football World Cup final, a Mini Cooper 'S' with floral designed bodywork or the psychedelic paint job on an old Dormobile van. These are just a few of the countless things that can trigger memories and transport us back in time to a bygone age that seems like only yesterday.

What was so special about the 1960s? Well, there were so many new and exciting things happening all at once, particularly in the areas of popular music and fashion. You can't help but remember how extraordinary it was to witness the scenes of fan hysteria that surrounded The Beatles when they first started to become famous. The amazing idolatry frenzy that they stirred up in their fans wherever they went became known as Beatlemania, and the four lads from Liverpool quickly became known as the 'Fab Four'. Their music and persona gripped the imagination of an entire generation and they became one of the most important elements of the 'swinging sixties'. Yes, The Beatles were big icons and an amazing phenomenon, significantly influencing world culture in that decade and for many decades thereafter. But the British cultural revolution was already well under way by the time The Beatles had their first hit record with *Love Me Do* in October 1962. Prior to that, The Beatles were known only to the local fans in their native

Sheet music books for songs by two of the 1960s' best loved groups, The Beatles' *I Feel Fine* (1964), and The Dave Clark Five's *Glad All Over* (1963).

Liverpool and to regulars at the Hamburg clubs that they had performed in. While The Beatles were still scratching a living in German nightclubs, several avant-garde British entrepreneurs and talented original artists were already well on course to help make the decade a very special one.

Mary Quant in London's Kings Road and John Stephen in Carnaby Street were already leading the fashion revolution with their clothes boutiques. And Vidal Sassoon was by then an established Bond Street hairdresser experimenting with new cuts and techniques in modern hairdressing. Meanwhile, Terence Conran was a successful designer and manufacturer of modern furniture, making

plans to open a huge new concept furniture and home accessories shop that would epitomise his vision of the 1960s lifestyle. The first of his Habitat stores subsequently opened on Fulham Road in London on 11 May 1964.

As well as being hugely successful recording artists, Elvis Presley and Cliff Richard had already become film stars, and Joe Meek had successfully created his now famous Holloway Road *Wall of Sound* and produced his first number one hit record, *Johnny Remember Me*, sung by John Leyton. Helen Shapiro had recorded hits at the now famous Abbey Road Studios in London, and at the age of 14 was the youngest female chart topper in the UK. Bands like the Rolling Stones, the Dave Clark Five, Manfred Mann, Brian Poole and the Tremeloes, and the Yardbirds had all been going for a while and were building large followings of fans around the London area, while other soon-to-be-famous 'Merseybeat' bands like Gerry and the Pacemakers and the Searchers were also successfully developing their pop music careers in and around Liverpool. Yes, The Beatles were amazing. Their music was, and still is, great, but there were many other 1960s groundbreaking talents that also contributed to the massive changes in world culture that we saw happen during the decade that was dubbed 'the swinging sixties' – a time when the word 'swinging' still had an innocent meaning: to be lively and exciting. In 1960, all over the country, there were many new revolutionary talents bubbling under the surface and about to explode onto the wider cultural scene. These innovative and talented people would go on to create a myriad of fresh delights in the form of music, fashion and entertainment, which would prove to be long lasting and that we would all continue to enjoy for decades to come.

Popular Music

There were a lot of different styles in popular music around, many having been carried over from previous generations, like jazz, blues, big band, rock and roll, doo-wop, skiffle, gospel, country and western, and folk music, but there was also a lot of new music being produced, like the Mersey Sound or Merseybeat, Tamla Motown, soul, Bluebeat, surfin', psychedelic and progressive rock, hard rock (heavy metal), bubblegum music and what was dubbed folk-pop, which was often the genre used by protest singers such as Bob Dylan, Joan Baez and Barry McGuire.

Throughout the sixties, the British popular music charts displayed a hotchpotch of vastly different tastes, indicating that people of all ages were buying their favourite records in large numbers; from Winifred Atwell and Frankie Vaughan to the Animals and the Zombies, with a few surprises also thrown into the mix like, for instance, Benny Hill, Napoleon XIV, and The Singing Nun. Ballads and easy-listening records were ever-present in the top twenty, with artists like Cliff Richard, Elvis Presley, Jim Reeves, Roy Orbison, the Seekers, the Bachelors, Engelbert Humperdinck and Tom Jones regularly selling huge numbers of such records. Much of what the charts contained didn't actually reflect the tastes of the younger generation. There was an underground music scene that had emerged from the mod clubs, where rare and hard-to-get American soul and rhythm & blues dance music was all the rage, but because of their limited availability many of these popular records didn't even get into the British top twenty. Lots of American artists, including Tommy Tucker, Dobie Gray,

The dance craze, 'the twist', took Britain by storm in late 1961 when Chubby Checker's *Let's Twist Again* became a UK chart hit. Soon, several twist records were released by a number of artists, including Sam Cooke with *Twistin' the Night Away* in early 1962. And there was even this twist record released in 1962 by Victor Silvester, the old-time musician and dance orchestra leader.

and P.P. Arnold were being added to the already long list of American mod favourites, like Muddy Waters and John Lee Hooker. If you couldn't find the American imports to buy legitimately in record shops then they were borrowed from friends and tape-recorded. There were several British bands and singers that were also considered to be part of the mod culture, like Steve Marriott and the Small Faces, and Chris Farlowe.

As far as the British popular music charts were concerned, The Beatles had the most consecutive number one hit records of any artist during the 1960s, with eleven number ones in a row from 1963–66, *From Me to You* through to *Yellow Submarine/Eleanor Rigby*. They then had six hits in a row from 1967–69 with *All You Need is Love* through to *The Ballad of John and Yoko*. Next came the Rolling Stones who managed five in a row from 1964–65 with *It's All Over Now* through to *Get Off of My Cloud*. Equalling the Rolling Stones with five in a row was Elvis Presley with *Little Sister/His Latest Flame* through to *Return to Sender* in 1961–62.

One hit wonders:

1960	*Tell Laura I Love Her* – Ricky Valance
1962	*Nut Rocker* – B. Bumble and the Stingers
1966	*Michelle* – The Overlanders
1968	*Fire* – Crazy World of Arthur Brown
1969	*In the Year 2525* – Zager and Evans
1969	*Je t'aime … moi non plus* – Jane Birkin and Serge Gainsbourg
1969	*Sugar Sugar* – The Archies

Straight into the charts at number one:

3 Nov 1960   *It's Now or Never* – Elvis Presley
11 Jan 1962   *The Young Ones* – Cliff Richard
23 Apr 1969   *Get Back* – The Beatles

Big names that never had a UK number one hit single:

Billy Fury
Brenda Lee
The Who
The Temptations
The Drifters
Mr Acker Bilk (although *Stranger on the Shore* was the biggest selling single of 1962, it only reached number two in the UK charts)

Instrumentals reaching number one in the charts:

(It is interesting to note that there were none from 1963–68 when the groups dominated the charts.)

1960   *Apache* – The Shadows
1961   *On the Rebound* – Floyd Cramer
1961   *Kon-Tiki* – The Shadows
1962   *Wonderful Land* – The Shadows
1962   *Nut Rocker* – B. Bumble and the Stingers
1962   *Telstar* – The Tornados
1963   *Dance On* – The Shadows
1963   *Diamonds* – Jet Harris and Tony Meehan (both former members of the Shadows)
1963   *Foot Tapper* – The Shadows
1968   *The Good, The Bad and The Ugly* – Hugo Montenegro Orchestra
1969   *Albatross* – Fleetwood Mac

Typical mid-sixties look that young girls would try to copy.

British entries in the Eurovision Song Contest and position:

1960	*Looking High High High* – Bryan Johnson	2nd
1961	*Are You Sure?* – The Allisons	2nd
1962	*Ring-A-Ding Girl* – Ronnie Carroll	Joint 4th
1963	*Say Wonderful Things* – Ronnie Carroll	4th
1964	*I Love the Little Things* – Matt Monro	2nd
1965	*I Belong* – Kathy Kirby	2nd
1966	*A Man Without Love* – Kenneth McKellar	9th
1967	*Puppet on a String* – Sandie Shaw	1st
1968	*Congratulations* – Cliff Richard	2nd
1969	*Boom Bang-a-Bang* – Lulu	Joint 1st

Mods and Rockers

Whenever post-war baby boomers find themselves reminiscing about events of the sixties with friends, they are inevitably asked: 'Were you a mod or a rocker?' There is always an assumption that you were one or the other, even if only through your taste in music. The smartly dressed mods listened and danced to R&B, Motown, Bluebeat, pop and blues records, whereas the leather-jacketed rockers, as their name suggests, preferred rock and roll music. Of course, most kids growing up in the 1960s were too young at the time to actually be a mod or a rocker, but many still had their own preferences when it came to fashion, style and music. Perhaps in your own childhood you aspired to become a mod when you got a bit older, but instead, as a 1970s teenager, you found yourself proudly sporting the

Date dress to knit in a cotton lace stitch

Knitmaster

FOR USE ON THE 302 AUTOMATIC   PRICE **1s.**

Girls of all ages attempted to make their own clothes to follow fashion. This was a typical dressmaking pattern book for a cotton lace stitch dress to make on a Knitmaster home knitting machine.

latest fashion in platform shoes, loon pants and knitted tank tops. Where did it all go wrong?

There has always been a lot of media emphasis put on the violence of mods and rockers, but in the scale of things it was only a relatively small number that took part in the fighting and rioting that made headline news. The mods played a big part in Britain's fashion and music culture and the majority of them steered clear of any confrontation or violence. Some mods did have customised motor-scooters, but it was not an essential element of the mod lifestyle. Whereas motorbikes were a big part of the rockers' daily life, for mods it was the clothes that were their main priority. The two groups were easily identifiable by their differing styles of dress. In simple terms, mods wore smart casual or formal clothes with clean and neatly cut hair, while rockers wore leather jackets and jeans with long, swept back hair. Many mods spent all their spare money on clothes, records and frequenting mod clubs and pubs. It was their passion, and some would even go without food so that they could buy some new items of mod clothing each week. There was no such thing as a credit card in Britain until the Barclaycard was introduced in 1966, and even then they weren't available to young people, so they had to have the cash in their pocket before they could buy anything. Most mods didn't have, or even want, a motor-scooter. Their clothes were far too valuable to risk ruining them by riding around in all weathers on a scooter. Most preferred to use other forms of covered transport – fashionable, if at all possible – like their own Mini Cooper S car.

The Hippies

The 1967 summer of love and the hippy fashion and life-style associated with it still gets a lot of publicity today. The hippy movement had been building up in Britain since the mid-sixties, but it was the San Francisco outdoor 'Human Be-In' or 'Happening' in January 1967 that sparked the San Francisco 'Summer of Love' that also hit Britain in the warm summer of that year. But, contrary to popular belief, in the late sixties not everyone dressed in kaftans and beads, nor did they wear flowers in their hair; most young people were still wearing Fred Perry polo shirts, faded Levi jeans and sneakers. We all loved those summer of 1967 'peace and love' records, such as Scott McKenzie's *San Francisco (Flowers in Your Hair)*, The Flowerpot Men's *Let's Go to San Francisco* and The Beatles' *All You Need is Love*, but the wearing of cowbells was strictly reserved for a few 'far-out' hippies, sitting cross-legged on some faraway cloud making daisy-chains. While all of that 'peace and love' business was going on, most people in Britain were still singing along to Petula Clark and Engelbert Humperdink songs, and listening to the Archers on the radio.

Cinema

Do you remember Pathé News and its wonderfully rousing theme music with the crowing cockerel? And those huge framed pictures of film stars that adorned the foyer walls and hung above the red-carpeted staircases in local cinemas everywhere? Do you remember standing for the National

Anthem when the film ended and staying until it finished playing? Going to the pictures was everyone's favourite outing. All those wonderful 1960s films: *One Hundred and One Dalmatians* (1961), *Dr No* (1962), *The Great Escape* (1963), *Goldfinger* (1964), *The Pink Panther* (1964), *A Fistful of Dollars* (1964), *A Hard Day's Night* (1964), *Mary Poppins* (1964), *Help!* (1965), *The Sound of Music* (1965), *2001: A Space Odyssey* (1968), *Born Free* (1966), *Bullet* (1968), *Chitty Chitty Bang Bang* (1968), *The Dirty Dozen* (1967), *Doctor Dolittle* (1967), *The Jungle Book* (1967), *Oliver!* (1968) and *Where Eagles Dare* (1969). There were just too many to list them all. Then there were all the great actors, many of whom are sadly no longer with us; people like Richard Burton (d.1984), Cary Grant (d.1986), Audrey Hepburn (d.1993), Charlton Heston (d.2008), Lee Marvin (d.1987), Steve McQueen (d.1980), David Niven (d.1983), Gregory Peck (d.2003), Peter Sellers (d.1980), John Wayne (d.1979) and Natalie Wood (d.1981) – to name but a few.

For children, it was Saturday Morning Pictures that provided the best fun. If you lived anywhere near a cinema you would have experienced the great joy of going along every Saturday morning to watch your screen heroes. Two or three hundred unruly children would descend upon anxious cinema commissionaires for two or three hours of film and live variety entertainment. There were no grown-ups, just kids up to the age of about 12 or 13, and it was the absolute highlight of any week. You will probably remember the cinema manager having to stop the film and threaten to send you all home if you didn't behave, and all the kids booing when the screen went blank while the projectionist changed reels. The solitary usherette would run for cover!

007

JAMES BOND

IN FOCUS
3/6

Souvenir James Bond 007 'In Focus' brochure from 1964, the year that the
film *Goldfinger* was released in the UK.

It was controlled mayhem, with the stalls and circle areas filled with kids cheering for the goodies and booing the baddies. There were lots of short films, mainly westerns, that seemed to consist of endless chases on horseback. The daring adventures of the Lone Ranger and Zorro, and the slapstick comedy of Mr Pastry would feature every week. Then there were the classic Charlie Chaplin and Buster Keaton films that had everyone in fits of laughter. And who can forget those wonderful old Shirley Temple films they used to show? During the interval there would be all sorts of competitions, from yo-yo tricks, hula hoop and juggling contests, to singing and dancing, with knockout rounds each week that led to the grand final. Most cinemas had their own club, especially the big groups of cinemas, and you would have a club badge and be made to sing the club song each week. Whether you belonged to the ABC Minors, Empire Rangers or the Granadiers Club, you definitely will have enjoyed every minute you spent at Saturday Morning Pictures.

Six

RADIO

You've been in bed for over an hour and you're still not sleepy. You managed to sneak your mum's small transistor radio into bed with you and you've got your head tucked well down beneath the bedcovers listening to Radio Luxembourg. The reception is particularly bad tonight, it's fading in and out more frequently than usual and you are missing all the best bits of the records. To top it all, the disc jockey has just faded out the Dave Clark Five's latest record, *Bits and Pieces*, to make way for the advertisements. Oh no! It's Horace Batchelor again, flogging the secret to his 'Famous Infra-Draw Method' of winning the football pools – 'and remember, that's Keynsham, spelt K-E-Y-N-S-H-A-M, Bristol'. It's hopeless! Having to contend with Radio Luxembourg's irregular transmission signal is hard

enough, but there are so many boring advertisements, and after suffering all of that, you only manage to catch snippets of your favourite records. The frustration eventually gets the better of you and you switch the radio off. You can now free your head from underneath the tangled bedclothes and come up for some air. Blimey, it was hot under there! In your annoyance, you slam the transistor radio down on top of the bedside cabinet and give your pillow a hefty thump with the palm of your hand to make a suitable dent for your head to rest in.

When you wake up the next morning, Easter Sunday, 29 March 1964, you reach out for mum's transistor radio and turn it on, but the Radio Luxembourg station closed down during the night and won't be back on again until their evening broadcasts later in the day. You twiddle the tuning knob in the hope that you might find something other than solemn classical music, boring news or religious programmes. To your absolute astonishment and delight you manage to pick up a radio station on a waveband where there was previously only a hissing noise, and this radio station is playing pop music, and during the day! It's the Rolling Stones' new record, *Not Fade Away*. You can't believe it, they actually let the record play right through to the very end, and when it does finally finish you discover that, at long last, your prayers have been answered. That very morning, a new commercial radio station, Radio Caroline, had started transmitting pop music from a ship off the coast of Felixstowe, south-east England. At last, there is a radio station playing pop music all day long, and they have lots of zany young disc jockeys to cheer you up; not at all like the old stuffed shirt presenters on the BBC.

Radio (the 1960s Transformation)

If you were around in the early 1960s, you will remember those boring times when you were stuck indoors on cold, wet winter days or when you were off school sick. There was very little daytime television back then and so the radio was usually left on in the background. During the week, apart from *Listen with Mother*, which was for little kids, most of the programmes were aimed at housewives and there was hardly anything on the radio to entertain the older kids and teenagers. You had to make do with programmes like *Housewives' Choice*, *Mrs Dale's Diary*, *Music While You Work*, *Woman's Hour*, and *Workers' Playtime*. The sixties had arrived and everything else around you was really beginning to liven up, but the radio programmes were still so old fashioned. There were a few good pop music and comedy programmes on BBC Radio at the weekends, and Radio Luxembourg would broadcast pop music in the evenings, but there was a big void in the middle. And, if you didn't have a television licence, you had to buy a special licence to listen to the radio; it cost £1 until 1964 and then it was increased to £1 5s, and you needed a separate licence again if you had a car radio.

The famous Radio Luxembourg, broadcasting on 208 metres on the medium-wave band, was one of the earliest commercial radio stations broadcasting to Britain (1933–92); it helped pioneer modern radio presentation styles and kick-started the careers of many well-known radio and television celebrities. The 1960s presenters and disc jockeys included such names as Pete Brady, Tony Brandon, Paul Burnett, Dave Cash, Simon Dee, Noel Edmonds, Keith Fordyce, Alan 'Fluff' Freeman, Stuart Grundy, Jack Jackson,

David Jacobs, Brian Matthew, Pete Murray, Jimmy Savile, Tommy Vance, Jimmy Young, and Muriel Young.

It was the wealthy Irish entrepreneur, Ronan O'Rahilly, who freed us from the shackles of BBC Radio and Radio Luxembourg when he launched Radio Caroline, the first UK offshore commercial radio station, on that Easter Sunday morning in 1964. It was the day that British radio broadcasting changed forever, and it happened in the sixties! Soon, lots of different offshore pirate radio stations were starting up and broadcasting from sites all round the British coastline: Radio Atlanta, 'Wonderful' Radio London (Big L), Radio Sutch (later became Radio City), Radio Invicta (later became King Radio and then Radio 390), Radio Pamela, Radio Essex (later became BBMS), Radio Scotland, Radio York/Radio 270, 'Swinging' Radio England and Britain Radio. The pirate radio stations had huge numbers of listeners and they made high street shopping come alive, with shop staff all over the country tuning in and forcing customers to listen at full volume. It was great for kids to grow up listening to those early pirate radio stations. They became one of the main components of the 'swinging sixties'.

By 1966 there were many commercial radio stations transmitting to different parts of the country, and that year a national opinion poll found that 45 per cent of the population was listening to the offshore stations and Radio Luxembourg. However, some of the offshore stations weren't successful and had to close down, while the others were eventually forced to shut when the Marine Broadcasting Offences Act came into effect at midnight on 14 August 1967. This paved the way for BBC Radio

to split its old BBC Light Programme into two services, thereby launching Radio 1 and Radio 2 in September 1967 – although not before hiring several of the most popular pirate radio disc jockeys to front the new pop music radio shows. Of course, being on the BBC the disc jockeys were reined in a bit and could no longer say whatever they wanted, as they had done on the defunct pirate stations. Kids moaned that the new BBC Radio 1 programme didn't play as many records as the pirate stations and there was now too much irrelevant chat, but the good news was that there were no advertisements on BBC Radio.

Many of the 1960s pirate radio disc jockeys went on to achieve greater fame following the demise of offshore radio. These include: Tony Blackburn, who was the first disc jockey to be heard on Radio 1 when it was launched on 30 September 1967, Dave Cash, Simon Dee (d.2009), Kenny Everett (d.1995), John Peel (d.2004), Emperor Rosko, Keith Skues, Ed 'Stewpot' Stewart, Dave Lee Travis, Tommy Vance (d.2005) and Johnnie Walker.

BBC Radio Programmes

Listening to radio was very popular throughout the 1960s, and although BBC Radio lost a proportion of its listener audience to offshore radio stations from 1964–67, the BBC still had a lot of well-liked radio programmes on the air. Not all were popular with the young, but the BBC did broadcast an enormous variety of comedy, drama and music programmes. Here is a selection of popular BBC Radio shows of the 1960s to stir the old grey cells:

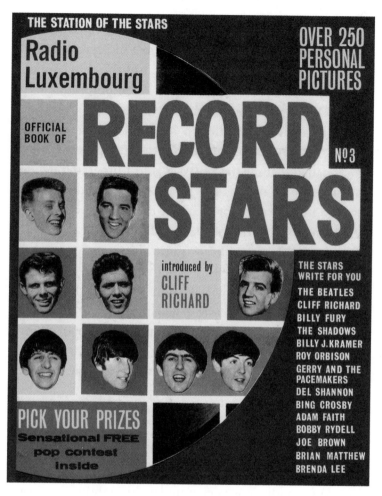

Until the arrival of offshore pirate radio in March 1964, Radio Luxembourg was the only English-language commercial radio station that could be heard in the UK. This Radio Luxembourg annual came out in 1964.

Any Answers? (1960s–present): BBC Light Programme, transferring to BBC Radio 2 and Radio 4 in 1967. Broadcast on Thursdays, listeners were invited to add their comments to the views expressed in the previous Friday's *Any Questions?* programme.

Any Questions? (1948–present): BBC Light Programme, transferring to BBC Radio 2 in 1967. Broadcast on Friday and repeated on BBC Radio 4 on Saturday at 1.15 p.m. A topical debate programme, chaired by Freddie Grisewood (1948–67) and David Jacobs (1967–83), in which a panel of four politicians and other public figures answered questions put to them by a studio audience.

The Archers (1951–present): BBC Light Programme, BBC Home Service and BBC Radio 4 from 1967. 'An everyday story of country folk.' First main broadcast was in January 1951. This is the world's longest running radio soap, now broadcast on BBC Radio 4. According to the BBC's press office in 2006, it remained BBC Radio 4's most popular non-news programme. In the 1960s, the story revolved around the Archer family of Brookfield farm near the village of Ambridge. Much of the action took place at the farm or in *The Bull* pub in the village. Some of the main early characters were Dan and Doris Archer, Jack and Peggy Archer, Phil Archer, Jack Woolley, Tom and Pru Forrest, John Tregorran and, of course, that old favourite – 'Well me old pal, me old beauties' – Walter Gabriel. Who could ever forget the happy-go-lucky 'maypole dance' theme tune entitled *Barwick Green*?

Beyond Our Ken (1958–64): BBC Light Programme. This comedy show was the predecessor to *Round the Horne* (1965–68); it starred Kenneth Horne, Kenneth Williams,

Betty Marsden, Hugh Paddick and Bill Pertwee. Barry Took and Eric Merriman wrote the scripts together up until the end of series three, then Barry Took left and Eric Merriman stayed on to write series four (October 1960) to series seven (November 1964), when the series ended. Douglas Smith played the very formal announcer.

The Billy Cotton Bandshow (1949–68): BBC Light Programme, transferred to Radio 2 in 1967. The dreaded shout of Billy Cotton's 'Wakey! Wakey!' each Sunday afternoon sent a shiver down every child's spine – and it was repeated on Wednesday evenings. This music and comedy show, presented by the larger than life bandleader, Billy Cotton, also featured Alan Breeze, Doreen Stephens and Kathie Kay. Its lifespan indicates that it was very popular with listeners, but it's unlikely there was ever a poll done of children's views.

Breakfast Show, Radio 1 (referred to in the 1960s *Radio Times* magazines as *The Daily Disc Delivery*) (1967–present): BBC Radio 1, 7–9 a.m. each weekday morning. Presented by Tony Blackburn from 30 September 1967 to 1 June 1973, and always referred to by him as *The Tony Blackburn Show*. It was the first show to be broadcast on Radio 1 when it went on air in 1967, and the first complete record to be played on the show was *Flowers in the Rain* by The Move, one of many songs synonymous with the 1967 'Summer of Love' and the 'Flower Power' period. The *Breakfast Show* was the most prized slot on BBC Radio 1, and still is today.

Breakfast Special (1960s): Radio 2. Broadcast each weekday morning 5.33–9 a.m. Presented by Paul Hollingdale with resident bands, singers, and records. Live music at half-past five in the morning!

Children's Favourites (1954–67): BBC Light Programme. Every Saturday morning Derek McCulloch (Uncle Mac) would play a selection of children's record requests. Starting each programme with the words, 'Hello children, everywhere!' McCulloch presented the programme until 1965, after which several presenters, including Leslie Crowther, presented the show until the launch of Radio 1 in 1967. Then it was renamed *Junior Choice* with Crowther as its first presenter until Ed 'Stewpot' Stewart took over in 1968.

Children's Hour (1922–64): BBC Home Service. Broadcast from 5–6 p.m. on weekdays. Filled with stories, plays and drama serials, as well as informative talks, children's newsreels and competitions. Featured presenters included Derek McCulloch, 'Uncle' Arthur Burrows, 'Auntie' Violet Carson, Jon Pertwee and Wilfred Pickles. Popular serials included *Jennings at School*, *Just So Stories for Little Children*, *Sherlock Holmes*, *Worzel Gummidge* and *Winnie the Pooh*. News that the programme was to end in March 1964 was met with a flood of letters to the BBC, a 'save Children's Hour' campaign and was even questioned in the House of Commons.

The Clitheroe Kid (1957–72): BBC Light Programme, transferring to Radio 2 and Radio 4 in 1967. This was a long-running situation comedy programme, featuring the diminutive Northern comedian, Jimmy Clitheroe, who played the part of a cheeky schoolboy. Amazingly, Jimmy Clitheroe was 50 years old when the show finally ended in 1972.

The Dales (see *Mrs Dale's Diary*).

Does the Team Think? (1957–76): BBC Light Programme, transferring to Radio 2 in 1967. Broadcast on Sunday afternoons and repeated on Monday evenings. It involved

McDonald Hobley in the chair and a panel made up of Jimmy Edwards, Ted Ray, Tommy Trinder and Leslie Crowther.

Easy Beat (1959–67): BBC Light Programme. Sunday mid-morning show produced and presented by Brian Matthew; it was recorded before a live audience at the Playhouse Theatre, just off Trafalgar Square in London. It featured the Johnny Howard Band and Kenny Ball's Jazzmen. Many famous bands and artists appeared as guests on the show, including Bert Weedon, Cilla Black and The Beatles. The growing success of pirate radio from 1964 onwards caused listening figures to drop and *Easy Beat* was finally axed when BBC Radio 1 was launched in 1967.

Family Choice (1967–70): BBC Radio 1 and Radio 2. Weekday 9–10 a.m. record request show. Gay Byrne was one of its regular presenters.

Family Favourites (1950s–1980): BBC Light Programme, transferring to Radio 1 and Radio 2. A record request show with Michael Aspel linking friends and relatives around the world with their favourite records.

Gardeners' Question Time (1947–present): BBC Home Service, transferring to Radio 4 in 1967. Broadcast on Sunday afternoons with Franklin Engelmann as the question master and a panel of experts to answer gardening questions put by members of the public.

Have A Go (1946–67): BBC Light Programme. A travelling radio quiz, hosted by Yorkshireman Wilfred Pickles, the first BBC newsreader to speak with a broad Yorkshire accent. Accompanied by his wife Mabel, Wilfred took the programme to church halls all round the country, challenging ordinary people to 'have a go' and answer quiz questions

for cash prizes. With 'Mabel at the table', Wilfred coined several catchphrases, including 'How do, how are yer?', 'Are yer courting?' to the younger contestants, and 'Give 'em the money, Mabel!' when they won, but all contestants were given the money anyway. Harry Hudson was the resident pianist in the early sixties and Eric James took over in 1966. The theme tune was *Have a Go, Joe* by Jack Jordan.

Housewives' Choice (1946–67): BBC Light Programme. A popular record request programme for women at home during the day, but it was mainly men that presented the shows, with the most popular presenter probably being George Elrick, known as 'The Smiling Face of Radio'. He would sign off each show with the words: 'This is Mrs Elrick's wee son George saying thanks for your company – and cheerio!' The signature tune was *In Party Mood* by Jack Strachey.

The Jimmy Young Show (1967–73): BBC Radio 1 and Radio 2, and Radio 2 (1973–2002). *The Jimmy Young Show* was on each weekday morning at 10–12 a.m. in the sixties; a show in which Jimmy played records, sang songs, greeted guests and spoke to people on the phone.

Junior Choice (1967–82): BBC Radio 1. A Saturday morning show of children's record requests first presented by Leslie Crowther. It replaced the old BBC Light Programme's *Children's Favourites* when Radio 1 was launched in 1967. Ed 'Stewpot' Stewart took over in 1968 and was the show's host until 1980, when Tony Blackburn replaced him. By then the show was seen as somewhat old fashioned and *The Tony Blackburn Saturday Show* replaced it in 1982.

The Likely Lads (1967–69): BBC Light Programme, transferring to BBC Radio 2 in September 1967. Radio

adaptation of the television comedy series created and written by Dick Clement and Ian La Frenais, and starring James Bolam and Rodney Bewes as Terry Collier and Bob Ferris. The sitcom show followed the friendship of two working-class young men in the north-east of England, in the mid-1960s. These episodes were originally made for television in 1964–66.

Midday Spin (1960): BBC Radio 1 and Radio 2. On each weekday at 12–1 p.m., various disc jockeys presented the show and played the latest records.

Mrs Dale's Diary (1948–69): BBC Light Programme, transferring to Radio 2 from 1967. Renamed *The Dales* in 1962, this was the first post-war daily weekday soap on British radio. It centred on the fictional life of Mrs (Mary) Dale, the wife of a doctor (Jim), and her family life at Virginia Lodge in the fictional London suburb of Parkwood Hill in Middlesex. A new episode was broadcast each weekday afternoon, with a repeat the following morning. Ellis Powell played Mrs Dale up until 1963 when Jessie Matthews replaced her. This was essential comfort listening for kids off school sick.

Music While You Work (1940–67): BBC Light Programme. This half-hour show was broadcast each weekday morning and afternoon. For many years it featured a different live band or orchestra playing a non-stop medley of popular tunes, but pre-recorded material was introduced in 1963. It was one of the programmes that were axed when the old BBC Light Programme ended in 1967 and Radio 1 was launched. Its signature tune was *Calling All Workers* by Eric Coates.

The Navy Lark (1959–77): BBC Light Programme, transferring to BBC Radio 2 in 1967. One of the longest-

running comedy radio shows ever. It was a send-up of the Senior Service (Royal Navy – oldest of the British armed services), and was about life aboard a fictional Royal Navy frigate called HMS *Troutbridge*. The 1960s cast included Stephen Murray as Lieutenant Murray (Number One), Leslie Phillips as Sub-Lieutenant Phillips, Jon Pertwee as Chief Petty Officer Pertwee and other characters, Richard Caldicott as Commander Povey, Heather Chasen as Wren Chasen and other characters, Ronnie Barker as Un-Able Seaman 'Fatso' Johnson and other characters, and Tenniel Evans as Able Seaman Taffy Goldstein and other characters. Laurie Wyman devised the series, and Tommy Reilly and James Moody composed the signature tune, *Trade Wind Hornpipe*. This show was thirty minutes of essential comedy listening every Sunday – 'Left hand down a bit!'

Paul Temple (1938–68): BBC Light Programme, transferring to Radio 4 in 1967. Based on the novels by Francis Durbridge, this fictional amateur detective, with the aid of his wife Steve, solved all sorts of crime mysteries. Several actors and actresses have portrayed the Temples over the years, but Peter Coke and Marjorie Westbury played the lead roles in the 1960s. This was another great mystery serial that had children captivated. The theme music, inspired by the rhythm of a train journey, was *Coronation Scot* by Vivian Ellis.

Pick of the Pops (1955–72): BBC Light Programme, transferring to BBC Radio 1 in 1967. A pop music programme based on the UK top-twenty singles chart. The show's best-known presenter, Alan 'Fluff' Freeman, took over from David Jacobs in 1961 and stayed until the programme ended in 1972. The signature tune for the show was *At the Sign of the Swinging Cymbal* by Brian Fahey and his orchestra.

Radio One O'Clock (1967–70): BBC Radio 1. Monday live music show presented by Rick Dane, with Johnny Howard and his band and regular singers Laura Lee, Danny Street and Tony Steven. There was always a guest artist or band.

Record Round Up (1948–68): BBC Light Programme, transferring to BBC Radio 1 and BBC Radio 2 from 1967. Former bandleader turned disc jockey, Jack Jackson, created this unusual pop record show where he interrupted pop records with excerpts from comedy monologues by comedians such as Shelley Berman and Bob Newhart. In the 1960s he recorded the radio shows from his home in Tenerife. His was the first fast-moving zany pop show on British radio, and was said to have inspired later presenters like Kenny Everett.

Round The Horne (1965–68): BBC Light Programme, transferring to BBC Radio 2 in 1967. This comedy show was created by Barry Took and Marty Feldman, and was the successor to *Beyond Our Ken*, which ran from 1958–64. It starred Kenneth Horne, Kenneth Williams, Betty Marsden, Hugh Paddick, Bill Pertwee and Douglas Smith. Popular sketches included *Fiona and Charles*, featuring Marsden and Paddick, and *Julian and Sandy*, featuring Paddick and Williams as two flamboyantly camp out-of-work actors. The fourth series, in 1968, was the last to be broadcast. A fifth series had been commissioned, but was abandoned after Horne's unfortunate death from a heart attack in February 1969.

Saturday Club (1958–69): BBC Light Programme, transferring to BBC Radio 1 in 1967. A live pop music show presented by Brian Matthew every Saturday morning. It

was essential listening for kids of all ages – that is if you weren't at Saturday Morning Pictures. The show included interviews with guest artists and pre-recorded live performances, as well as record requests and new releases. The programme followed on immediately after *Children's Favourites*, which meant that lots of young kids also got hooked on the show. Many home-grown pop stars of the day appeared on the show, including The Beatles (they appeared ten times during the early sixties), the Everly Brothers, the Bee Gees, Dusty Springfield, the Searchers, Jimi Hendrix, Manfred Mann, the Small Faces, Cream, The Who and many more. The cheery welcome of Brian Matthew's 'Hello my ol' mateys!' was a familiar greeting that could be heard in every hairdressers and barbers shop throughout the country each Saturday morning, with hairdressers everywhere reaching to fine-tune their radios for crystal-clear reception. The theme tune was Humphrey Littleton's *Saturday Jump*.

Savile's Travels (1968–69): Radio 1. Each Sunday afternoon at 2 p.m. Jimmy Savile introduced interviews and records from his weekly world of people, places and pop.

Semprini Serenade (1957–82): BBC Light Programme, transferring to BBC Radio 2 in 1967. This was another 'easy listening' weekday evening show that would send the kids running for cover! 'Old ones, new ones, loved ones, neglected ones' – Alberto Semprini played them all on keyboard and piano, accompanied by Harry Rabinowitz and the BBC Revue Orchestra (this became the BBC Radio Orchestra in 1964), and later, the Serenade Orchestra.

Sing Something Simple (1959–2001): BBC Light Programme, transferring to Radio 2 in 1967. A torturous half-

hour for any child forced to listen to this every Sunday evening, but its longevity proved that it must have been popular with older people. The show featured the Cliff Adams Singers performing a collection of non-stop familiar songs, accompanied by pianist and accordionist Jack Emblow and his quartet. The programme came to an end with the death of Cliff Adams in October 2001.

Today (1957–present): BBC Home Service, transferring to BBC Radio 4 in 1967. Early morning news and current affairs programme, presented by Jack de Manio throughout the 1960s, until 1971. You may remember listening to the dulcet tones of the hugely popular Jack de Manio and his roaming London reporter, Monty Modlyn, as you dipped your neatly cut bread soldiers into a boiled egg. You would, no doubt, have been late for school if you relied on Jack de Manio's time checks in the morning. He was notoriously gaffe-prone and often got the time wrong.

The Tony Blackburn Show (See *Breakfast Show, Radio 1*).

Top of the Form (1948–86): BBC Light Programme, transferring to BBC Radio 2 in 1967, and sometimes simulcast on BBC Radio 1. This was radio's general knowledge quiz show for teams of children from secondary schools around the country. However, it mainly featured pupils from grammar and independent schools. The 1960s presenters included John Ellison, Paddy Feeny, Tim Gudgin and Geoffrey Wheeler. The quiz involved teams from different age groups and it was very popular with young listeners eager to pit their wits against kids of their own age. The rousing theme music was taken from *Marching Strings* by Marshall Ross (a pseudonym of orchestra leader and composer Ray Martin).

Woman's Hour (1946–present): BBC Light Programme, transferring to Radio 2 in 1967, and then to Radio 4 in 1973. A weekday afternoon woman's magazine programme that was on from 2–3 p.m. each afternoon, until 1991 when it was moved to a morning slot. Norman Collins originally created the programme as a daily programme of music, advice and entertainment for women at home during the day. The 1960s presenters included Marjorie Anderson and Judith Chalmers. It was essential listening for mums at home in the afternoon, and another interesting radio show for kids off school with childhood illnesses, particularly boys, who would be fascinated by live discussions about women's menstrual problems and the menopause – they discussed such things on the radio as far back as 1947!

Workers' Playtime (1941–64): BBC Home Service, then Light Programme (1957–64). This was a radio variety touring show that was broadcast live three days a week from different factory canteens around the country, as selected by the Ministry of Labour. The programme was produced by Bill Gates and featured countless well-known entertainers, like Janet Brown, Charlie Chester, Peter Sellers, Tony Hancock, Frankie Howerd, Roy Hudd, Anne Sheldon, Betty Driver (now famous for her role as *Coronation Street's* barmaid, Betty Williams), Eve Boswell, Dorothy Squires, Arthur English, Julie Andrews, Morecambe and Wise, Bob Monkhouse, Ken Dodd, Ken – 'I won't take me coat off – I'm not stopping!' – Platt, Gert and Daisy (Elsie and Doris Waters), and the impressionist Peter Goodwright. Children who listened to the show imagined that working in a factory was fun and all about having a good time – what was so hard about that? The show was originally scheduled to

run for just six weeks, but went on to become one of the longest-running radio shows in history.

There were a lot of programme changes on Radio 1 and Radio 2 from their opening until 1970, and there were several shared programmes. Radio 2 struggled to find enough of its own core programmes to fill the airtime. Here is what you would have been listening to on Radio 1 if you had been at home on Tuesday 19 September 1968.

5.30 a.m.	News & Weather.
5.33	*Breakfast Special* (as Radio 2).
7.00	*The Tony Blackburn Show* with today's top discs and reviews.
9.00	*Family Choice* with Gay Byrne (as Radio 2).
10.00	*The Jimmy Young Show* with a mixture of discs and guests and phone calls.
12.00	*Midday Spin* with Tony Brandon.
1.00 p.m.	Don Moss with the *Disc Jockey Derby* show.
2.00	Dave Cash with records and live music.
4.15	*The David Symonds Show* playing records and talking to guests.
5.45	Chris Denning with *What's New* in pop records.
6.45	*Foreverett* presented by Kenny Everett.
7.30–10.00	(as Radio 2)
10.00	*Late Night Extra* presented by Pete Myers with music, news and guests.
12.00	Midnight Newsroom.
12.05	*Night Ride* presented by Bruce Wyndham, with swinging sounds on and off the record.
2.00	News & Weather
2.02	Closedown.

Radio 1 presenters and disc jockeys in the 1960s included: John Benson, Alan Black, Tony Blackburn, Tony Brandon, Gay Byrne, Dave Cash, Pat Doody, Pete Drummond, Tom Edwards, Kenny Everett, Chris Denning, Joe Loss, Ed Stewart, Keith Skues, David Symonds, Emperor Rosko, Robin Boyle, Pete Brady, Chris Denning, Peter Latham, Barry Mason, Brian Matthew, Pete Myers, Wally Whyton, John Peel, Don Moss, Pete Murray, Sean Kelly, The Baron, Stewart Henry, Mike Raven, Humphrey Lyttelton, David Jacobs, Terry Wogan (doing the *Late Night Extra* show back then), Dwight Whylie and Jimmy Young.

This was the BBC Radio 2 Schedule for 19 September 1968:

5.30 a.m.	News & Weather.
5.33	*Breakfast Special* presented by Paul Hollingdale with records and resident band.
9.00	*Family Choice* with Gay Byrne playing your record requests.
10.00	*The Jimmy Young Show* (as Radio 1).
11.00	*Morning Story.*
11.15	*The Dales.*
11.31	*Melody on the Move* with Jimmy Hanley presenting orchestral music.
12.00	*Midday Spin* with Tony Brandon (as Radio 1).
1.00 p.m.	Bruce Trent asks: *Do You Remember?* Musical memories.
2.00	*Woman's Hour* introduced by Marjorie Anderson.
2.45	*Woman's Hour Play* with the fourth instalment of *Rough Husband* by Patricia Campbell.
3.00	Dave Cash (as Radio 1).

4.15	*The Dales*.
4.31	Racing Results.
4.34	*Roundabout* with Robin Boyle presenting news, views, and music.
6.32	Sports Review.
6.40	Brian Matthew with *Album Time*, review of LPs and EPs.
7.30	*News Time* with Corbet Woodall.
7.45	*Top of the Form* with question masters John Ellison and Tim Gurgin.
8.15	Vince Hill says *Be My Guest*.
8.45	*The Likely Lads* – comedy with James Bolam and Rodney Bewes.
9.15	*Nights of Gladness* with the BBC Concert Orchestra.
10.00–2.02	(as Radio 1)

Radio 2 presenters and disc jockeys in the 1960s included: David Allan, Marjorie Anderson, Alan Black, Dave Cash, Ken Dodd, Pete Drummond, Tom Edwards, Bruce Wyndham, Kenneth Alwyn, Ronnie Aldrich, David Gell, Jimmy Hanley, Peter Latham, Barry Mason, George Martin, Brian Matthew, Wally Whyton, Charles Crathorn, Ken Dodd, Catherine Boyle, Robin Boyle, Eric Robinson, Bruce Trent, Elenid Williams and Jimmy Young.

Seven

TELEVISION

It seems incredible to think how much of children's lives revolved around television in the 1960s, considering that up until April 1964, when BBC2 was launched, there were only two channels broadcasting, BBC and ITV. There were no video or other recording machines around to enable you to record and watch programmes that you missed. If you weren't sitting in front of the screen when a programme was first shown, then that was it – you had missed it. It's amazing how many childhood memories are stirred by reminders of those old television programmes that you once rushed home from school to see, or begged mum and dad to let you stay up to watch. Kids didn't have television sets in their bedrooms back then, so you couldn't secretly watch a late night programme in the darkness of your room

with the sound turned down. Your parents had complete control over the television's power button, and they decided what you were allowed to watch and when. Mind you, there wasn't 24-hour television in those days, and popular programmes were usually shown within a short time frame in the evening. In the mid-1960s, even Saturday's television programmes didn't start until lunchtime, and then the afternoon was taken up with *Grandstand* on BBC1 and *World of Sport* on ITV. If you weren't into sport then you had to wait until 5.30 p.m. before the first real programme came on, and that was usually *Doctor Who* on BBC1. The BBC2 channel didn't come on air until 7.30 p.m. All three channels would usually close down after their late-night movies, which started around 11.30 p.m., but BBC1 didn't always show a late movie on a Saturday and would sometimes close down before midnight.

People who grew up in the 1960s will often say that they didn't watch much television when they were a kid because they were playing outside all the time. It is true that kids loved to play out and did spend as much time as possible outside, but after all these years, most still manage to vividly remember all of the old television programmes. After all, there were a lot of new groundbreaking programmes being made, and television itself was still a fairly new form of entertainment in many working-class homes, so it was still somewhat of a novelty. There are a number of 1960s television personalities that are no longer in the limelight, but are so synonymous with the period that even today people instinctively link them to the sixties. People like: Arthur Haynes (d.1966) – star of the very popular ITV comedy programme, *The Arthur Haynes Show*; Cathy McGowan –

known as 'Queen of the Mods', she was the most in-touch presenter of ITV's pop music show, *Ready Steady Go!*; Mick McManus – a professional wrestler who appeared in the wrestling segment of ITV's *World of Sport* on Saturday afternoons; Valerie Singleton – one of the main presenters of the BBC's children's programme, *Blue Peter*; Susan Stranks – one of the main presenters on ITV's children's programme, *Magpie*; Muriel Young (d.2001) – presenter of various children's television programmes on ITV (remember Pussy Cat Willum, Ollie Beak and Fred Barker?).

There were also loads of fictional television characters that we grew up with and remember so well from our favourite television shows of the 1960s. Characters like Minnie Caldwell – the timid friend of bossy Ena Sharples and fellow gossip Martha Longhurst in ITV's *Coronation Street*, played by Margot Bryant (d.1988); Little Joe Cartwright – one of the leading characters in the western series, *Bonanza*, played by schoolgirl heart-throb, Michael Landon (d.1991); Jason King - the flamboyant leading character played by Peter Wyngarde in the television series, *Department 'S'*; Napoleon Solo – the suave spy character in *The Man From U.N.C.L.E.* played by Robert Vaughn; Troy Tempest – the square-jawed puppet pilot of *Stingray*, the super fast submarine, in ITV's string-puppet television programme for children; Simon Templar – the leading character in the ITV series, *The Saint*, played by Roger Moore.

There were just too many popular television programmes to mention them all, but here is a selection that will surely bring back some fond memories:

77 Sunset Strip (1958–64): ITV. An American fictional private detective series that starred Efrem Zimbalist Jr as Stu

Bailey, and Roger Smith as Jeff Spencer, both former government secret agents. Edd Byrnes played the wisecracking, hair-combing, seriously cool valet parking attendant from next door, Gerald Lloyd Kookson III, known to all as 'Kookie', the wannabe investigator. The two private detectives worked out of offices at 77 Sunset Strip, next door to Dean Martin's real-life nightclub, *Dino's*. All the girls loved 'Kookie', and his frequent use of the comb lead to a huge increase in comb sales in Britain.

All Gas and Gaiters (1966–71): BBC1. An ecclesiastical situation comedy series set in the fictional St Ogg's Cathedral. The farcical stories were centred on rivalries between the resident clergy. Its stars included William Mervyn, Robertson Hare and Derek Nimmo.

Animal Magic (1962–83): BBC1. A children's television series presented by Johnny Morris, who often dressed as a zookeeper and always managed to find humorous ways of explaining animal facts to children, including lots of funny voice-overs. The series was a mixture of film location reports and animals brought into the studio. Most of the animal films were made at Bristol Zoo.

The Arthur Haynes Show (1956–66): ITV. A British comedy sketch series, starring the talented Arthur Hayes, best known for his famous portrayal of a tramp ('Up to me neck in muck and bullets!'), a character that was created by Johnny Speight. Other regulars on the show included Nicholas Parsons, Patricia Hayes, Graham Stark and Dermot Kelly who played another tramp called Irish. The series only ended because of Arthur Haynes' sudden death in 1966.

The Avengers (1961–69): ABC, then Thames Television for ITV. A British television adventure series created by Sydney

Newman about secret agents in 1960s Britain. The cast featured John Steed played by Patrick Macnee, Dr David Keel played by Ian Hendry (1961), Dr Cathy Gale played by Honor Blackman (1962–64), Emma Peel played by Diana Rigg (1965–68) and Tara King played by Linda Thorson (1968–69). The secret agent storylines often involved a lot of science fiction and fantasy that made it hard for kids to follow. In 1976–77, the series was revived as *The New Avengers* starring Patrick Macnee, Gareth Hunt and Joanna Lumley.

Batman (1966–68): ITV. The original American television series that starred Adam West and Burt Ward as Bruce Wayne (Batman) and Dick Grayson (Robin), two crime-fighting heroes who dressed up in tights and masks to defend the people of fictional Gotham City. There was a Batphone, Batcave and a Batmobile, and each episode included a major brawl (punctuated with words like 'POW!', 'ZOKK!' and 'BAM!' that appeared across the screen). Batman and Robin were always completely outnumbered, but the dynamic duo always won the day and saved the people of Gotham City from villains like the Joker, the Penguin, Catwoman and the Riddler.

Benny Hill Show (1955–68): BBC TV/BBC1 and (1957–60 & 1967) ATV for ITV. Benny Hill is probably best recognised for his later (1969–89) Thames Television series, but he was on television a lot in the 1960s performing his comedy sketches, slapstick and songs. He even did passable impersonations of people like Hughie Green and Alan Wicker. His 1960s shows were less smutty than the later ones. Henry McGee, Bob Todd, John 'Jackie' Wright and Nicholas Parsons were among the regular performers that appeared in his 1960s shows.

The Beverly Hillbillies (1963–72): ITV. An American situation comedy series about a hillbilly family that move to Beverly Hills when they become rich after finding oil on their land. The show starred Buddy Ebsen as Jed Clampett, Irene Ryan as Daisy May 'Granny' Moses, Donna Douglas as Elly May Clampett and Max Baer Jr as Big Jethro Bodine.

Bewitched (1964–72): BBC1. An American situation comedy series that starred Elizabeth Montgomery who played a young witch named Samantha, who meets and marries a mortal named Darrin Stephens (played by Dick York in the sixties). While Samantha pledges to forsake her powers and become a typical suburban housewife, her magical family disapprove of the mixed marriage and frequently interfere in the couple's lives. The chief antagonist was Samantha's mother Endora, played by Agnes Moorehead. Samantha would twitch her nose to perform one of her many spells, which were often intended to help her husband when he was in some difficulty.

Blue Peter (1958–present): BBC TV and BBC1. Nobody ever thought that *Blue Peter* would evolve into the programme it has become today, or that it would still be running over fifty years down the line. It was first aired on 16 October 1958, and then appeared as a weekly 15-minute programme that was aimed at 5- to 8-year-olds. The first two presenters were Christopher Trace and Leila Williams, winner of Miss Great Britain in 1957. In the programme, Christopher Trace would demonstrate boys' toys, such as model railways, aeroplanes and trains, and Leila Williams would show girls' toys, mainly dolls, and girls' hobbies. Occasionally, the artist Tony Hart would appear on the programme, using his drawings to tell children's stories. In the

The first *Blue Peter* book was published in 1964. These books (1966, 1967, 1965) show regular 1960s *Blue Peter* presenters John Noakes, Valerie Singleton and Christopher Trace with some of the early *Blue Peter* animals.

early years there were no *Blue Peter* badges, pets or ships, and no *Blue Peter* garden. In 1962, Leila Williams was removed from the programme by its newly-appointed producer and Anita West took over for a short time until Valerie Singleton was appointed in September 1962. Also in 1962, the first *Blue Peter* pet, Petra the mongrel dog, appeared on the show, but sadly the dog was sickly and died after just one appearance. A lookalike dog replaced her without viewers being told, and the new Petra continued to appear on the show until 1972. In 1963, the first *Blue Peter* badge was introduced, and that same year Fred the tortoise joined the show. From 1964, the programme's running time was extended to 25 minutes and it was shown twice a week, with a more wide-ranging content, including charity appeals and lots

of adventure and discovery features. That year, *Blue Peter* also got its first cat, Jason, a Seal Point Siamese. In 1965, Patch, son of Petra, became part of the team and remained there until 1971 when he died from a rare disease (Shep, a border collie, replaced him). In December 1965, John Noakes joined Singleton and Trace as one of the show's main presenters. In July 1967, Christopher Trace left and was replaced by Peter Purves. After that, Singleton, Noakes and Purves continued as the show's main presenters for the remainder of the sixties. The theme tune was a sea shanty called *Barnacle Bill*.

Bonanza (1959–73): ITV. A weekly western series based on the adventures of the Cartwright family and the goings-on at their 1,000 mile² fictional ranch called Ponderosa on the shore of Lake Tahoe in Nevada. The head of the family was Ben Cartwright, played by Lorne Green. He had three sons, each by a different wife, Adam (Pernell Roberts), Eric or 'Hoss' (Dan Blocker) and Joseph or 'Little Joe' (Michael Landon). Michael Landon was the only original leading cast member who was wig-free throughout the series.

Bronco (1958–62): BBC TV. An American western television adventure series starring Ty Hardin as Bronco Layne, a former Confederate officer who wandered the Old West encountering all sorts of famous names, from Billy the Kid to Theodore Roosevelt.

Cheyenne (1955–63): ITV. Made by Warner Brothers, this was the first hour-long American television western series. It starred Clint Walker as Cheyenne Bodie, a former frontier scout who became a drifter taking all sorts of short-term jobs on ranches, wagon trains and cattle drives. And he sometimes worked as a civilian Cavalry scout, a federal

marshal and a special investigator; an all-round hero who sorted out conflicts everywhere he went. Clint Walker was the only regular cast member but many well-known guests appeared, including Angie Dickinson, James Garner, Michael Landon and Rod Taylor.

Cilla (1968–69): BBC1. Cilla Black's own series of music shows in which she sang songs, danced and introduced guest artists. During the series her guests included Donovan, Georgie Fame, Tom Jones, Henry Mancini, Dusty Springfield and Ringo Starr. Paul McCartney (credited as 'Lennon/McCartney') wrote the theme song, *Step Inside Love*, which reached number eight in the UK charts in March 1968.

Coronation Street (1960–present): Granada Television for ITV. A prime time soap opera created by Tony Warren

Annuals of television series, like *Crackerjack, Emergency Ward 10* and *The Man from U.N.C.L.E.*, were very popular Christmas stocking fillers for children of all ages.

that was set and produced in Manchester, about life in and around the fictional Coronation Street. First broadcast on 9 December 1960, it was shown twice a week in the 1960s (three times a week from 1989 and five times a week from 2009). The 1960s cast included such characters as Ena Sharples (Violet Carson), Elsie Tanner (Patricia Phoenix), Annie Walker (Doris Speed), Mr Swindley (Arthur Lowe), Len Fairclough (Peter Adamson), Minnie Caldwell (Margot Bryant), Martha Longhurst (Lynne Carol), Ken Barlow (William Roache) and Albert Tatlock (Jack Howarth).

Crackerjack! (1955–84): BBC TV. A weekly children's comedy and variety show. 'It's Friday, it's five to five … It's Crackerjack!' Filmed in front of an audience of excited children, this was one of the most popular children's television programmes ever. The show's first presenter was Eamonn Andrews (1955–64), who mimed during the singing. Leslie Crowther took over from 1964–68, and then Michael Aspel became its presenter through to 1974. The regular performers included Ronnie Corbett, Joe Baker, Jack Douglas, Peter Glaze, Rod McLennan, Christine Holmes and Jillian Comber. And there were always one or two big name special guests who were often the top artists or groups of the day. You would definitely have run home from school to see this. It had everything you needed to help you forget a hard week: corny jokes, singalongs, pop star guests, games, quizzes, comedy sketches and 'Double or Drop', the game where kids' arms were loaded with prizes as they answered each question correctly or with cabbages if they got them wrong. They were out of the game if they dropped anything or if they got two questions wrong. Everyone that took part

got a *Crackerjack* pencil and it was an unwritten rule that whenever the presenter said 'Crackerjack', the audience would shout back loudly 'Crack-er-jack!'

Dad's Army (1968–77): BBC1. A British situation comedy about a Home Guard platoon based at the fictional seaside town of Walmington-on-Sea during the Second World War. Written by Jimmy Perry and David Croft, it starred Arthur Lowe as Captain Mainwaring (bank manager), John Le Mesurier as Sergeant Arthur Wilson (bank clerk), Clive Dunn as Lance-Corporal Jack Jones (butcher), James Beck as Private Joe Walker (local spiv), Ian Lavender as Private Frank Pike (junior bank clerk and 'stupid boy'), John Laurie as Private James Frazer (Scottish coffin maker), Arnold Ridley as Private Charles Godfrey (tailor and the platoon's medical orderly), Bill Pertwee as Chief ARP Warden William Hodges (grumpy greengrocer), Janet Davies as Mrs Mavis Pike (Private Pike's mother and Sergeant Wilson's lover), Frank Williams as Reverend Timothy Farthing (effeminate vicar), Edward Sinclair as Maurice Yeatman (the verger) and Colin Bean as Private Sponge (sheep farmer who sometimes spoke up for the rest of the platoon). Bud Flanagan sang the theme song, *Who Do You Think You Are Kidding Mr Hitler*, for which Jimmy Perry and Derek Taverner composed the music, with lyrics by Jimmy Perry.

Danger Man (1960–68): ATV for ITV. A British television drama series created by Ralph Smart about a fictional special security operative working for NATO, featuring undercover agent John Drake, played by Patrick McGoohan. The opening titles started with McGoohan's voice-over narration: 'Every government has its secret service branch. America, CIA; France, Deuxieme Bureau; England, MI5.

NATO also has its own. A messy job? Well that's when they usually call on me or someone like me. Oh yes, my name is Drake, John Drake.'

Dee Time (1967–69): BBC1. Early evening prime time television show with Simon Dee chatting to famous guests of the day. The show always opened with the announcement, 'It's S-i-i-i-mon Dee', and closed with a film shot of Dee driving away in an E-Type Jaguar with a blonde model sat next to him.

The Dick Emery Show (1963–81): BBC1. A comedy sketch series with Dick Emery donning many disguises to play fictional comic characters that became very familiar to viewers. Such characters included the buck-toothed Church of England vicar, a man-eating spinster called Hettie, a camp man who coined the phrase 'Hallo Honky Tonk' and a denim-clad bovver boy called Gaylord. One of Emery's best-loved catchphrases came from Mandy, the busty middle-aged peroxide-blonde woman who would always finish a conversation with the catchphrase, 'Ooh, you are awful … but I like you!' Then Mandy would give the interviewer a hefty shove and trip in her high heels as she walked away from him.

Dixon of Dock Green (1956–76): BBC TV. Saturday evening drama series featuring PC George Dixon, played by Jack Warner, who was an old-style London beat-bobby; solving crime using the soft touch, 'a nice cup of tea and a chat', with the odd 'clip around the ear' for the young tearaways. Jack Warner was 60 years old when the television series first started, but with all the success he had at solving crime, it still took until he was well past retirement age before he got promoted to the rank of sergeant. This

was something that mystified even the youngest of minds! 'Evenin' all!'

Doctor in the House (1969–70): LWT for ITV. A British comedy series about the misadventures of a group of medical students based at the fictional St Swithin's Hospital in London. The main characters were Michael Upton (played by Barry Evans), Duncan Waring (Robin Nedwell), Paul Collier (George Layton), Dick Stuart-Clark (Geoffrey Davies) and Professor Geoffrey Loftus (Ernest Clark).

Doctor Who (1963–89 and 2005–present): BBC1. A science fiction adventure series that was first broadcast by BBC TV on 23 November 1963. The programme follows the adventures of a fictional time-traveller known as 'the Doctor' who travels through space and time in his blue 1950s police-box, called the TARDIS. The original Doctor was played by William Hartnell (1963–66) followed by Patrick Troughton (1966–69). Since then there have been nine actors cast in the title role, making eleven in all. The Doctor has always travelled with at least one companion. His original companions were his granddaughter Susan Foreman (played by Carole Ann Ford), and school teachers Barbara Wright (Jacqueline Hill) and Ian Chesterton (William Russell). Other 1960s companions included Vicky (Maureen O'Brien), Steven Taylor (Peter Purves), Katarina (Adrianne Hill), Sara Kingdom (Jean Marsh), Dodo Chaplet (Jackie Lane), Polly (Anneke Wills), Ben Jackson (Michael Craze), Jamie McCrimmon (Frazer Hines), Victoria Waterfield (Deborah Watling) and Zoe Hariot (Wendy Padbury). The series features many monsters and villains, the most famous being the Daleks, which are tank-like mechanical casings that carry the mutated remains of the Kaled people of the

planet Skaro. When they first appeared in 1963, kids all over the country were ducking down behind sofas to hide from the scary monsters.

Double Your Money (1955–68): Rediffusion/ITV. A quiz show in which members of the public won cash prizes for answering increasingly difficult general knowledge questions, with the prize money doubling after each answered question. When the prize money reached £32 then contestants had to answer questions from inside a soundproofed sealed glass booth. Hughie Green was the host for the entire life of the show.

Emergency Ward 10 (1957–67): ITV. One of British television's first soap operas, and the first hospital-based drama on British television. It was about life behind the swing-doors of fictional Oxbridge General Hospital. Its stars included Jill Browne as Nurse Carole Young, Rosemary Miller as Nurse Pat Roberts, Elizabeth Kentish as Sister Cowley and Charles Tingwell as House Surgeon Alan Dawson.

The Expert (1968–76): BBC1. A British police drama series about a pathologist called Dr John Hardy who worked for the Home Office and would use his forensic knowledge to solve various cases. Marius Goring played the lead role. It was one of the first BBC dramas to be made in colour.

Father, Dear, Father (1968–73): Thames Television for ITV. A British situation comedy about a father (Patrick Glover played by Patrick Cargill) coping with the antics of his two teenage daughters, Ann and Karen, played by Natasha Pyne and Ann Holloway. He was aided by the girls' nanny, played by Noel Dyson.

Flipper (1964–67): ITV. Made by NBC in America, this was a children's television series about a bottlenose dol-

phin named Flipper who was the wild pet of Porter Ricks, Chief Warden at the fictional Coral Key Park and Marine Preserve in southern Florida, and his two sons Sandy and Bud. Flipper lived in a lagoon near the Ricks' cottage, and together with the Ricks family he helped protect the park and its wildlife inhabitants. Flipper was often instrumental in rescuing members of the family from dangerous situations and in apprehending criminals and mischief-makers in the park.

Forsyte Saga (1967–69): BBC2 and repeated on BBC1. This drama series was adapted from the novels by John Galsworthy. The series was about the life and times of a fictional leading upper-middle-class British family by the name of Forsyte. It starred Eric Porter as Soames, Kenneth More as Young Jolyon and Nyree Dawn Porter as Irene. The series was hugely popular and 18 million people tuned in to watch the final episode in 1969.

The Frankie Howerd Show (1964–66): BBC1. A comedy series written by Ray Galton and Alan Simpson, which was based on a mixture of chat and comedy sketches featuring Frankie Howerd. Regular cast members included John Le Mesurier and June Whitfield. There were lots of his seemingly off-the-cuff remarks to the audience and recurring catchphrases like 'Oooh, no missus', 'Oh well, please yourself' and 'Titter ye not'. But it was later found that everything, including the off-the-cuff remarks, was scripted.

George and the Dragon (1966–68): ATV for ITV. A situation comedy written by Vince Powell and Harry Driver. It starred Sid James as George Russell, an incorrigible letch of a chauffeur/handyman to Colonel Maynard (John Le Mesurier), and Peggy Mount as Miss Gabriel Dragon, a

bellowing battle-axe character who tried to keep George in check while he did everything he could to get rid of her.

Grandstand (1958–2007): BBC TV and BBC1. The first programme on British television to pull together a variety of sports into one show. Its first presenter was Peter Dimmock, but David Coleman took over the hot seat just a few weeks later, and he continued to present the show until 1968 when Frank Bough took over.

Gunsmoke (1955–75): ITV. Also produced under the titles of *Gun Law* and *Marshal Dillon*. A television western series starring James Arness in the lead role of Marshal Matt Dillon, Dennis Weaver as Chester Goode, Milburn Stone as Dr Galen 'Doc' Adams and Amanda Blake as Miss Kitty, owner of the fictional Long Branch Saloon in Dodge City, Kansas. Everyone remembers Dennis Weaver playing the limping Chester 'Mis-ter Dil-lon' Goode.

Hancock's Half Hour (1956–69): BBC TV. This was the television version of the popular radio comedy series. As with the radio series, it starred Tony Hancock as Anthony Aloysius St John Hancock, who continually failed in his attempts to rise above his humble origins. Sid James was the only other cast member to transfer across from radio, although Kenneth Williams and Hattie Jacques did make some guest appearances. Liz Frazer, Irene Handl, Hugh Lloyd, John Le Mesurier, Warren Mitchell, Arthur Mullard and Richard Wattis also made guest appearances. Wally Scott composed the distinctive tuba-based theme.

I Love Lucy (1955–65): ITV. One of the first ever family situation comedies shown on ITV when the new channel started in 1955. It starred Lucille Ball as Lucy Ricardo, the

scatty wife of singer/bandleader Ricky Ricardo, played by Lucy's real-life husband, Desi Arnaz. In the series, Lucy got herself into all sorts of madcap situations with friends and landlords Ethel Mertz, played by Vivian Vance, and Fred Mertz, played by William Frawley. This was one of the funniest shows on television. Kids and grown-ups loved it!

Juke Box Jury (1959–67): BBC TV and BBC1. A pop music panel show in which the host, DJ David Jacobs, played excerpts from the latest pop records and the four celebrity jury made comments and voted the record a 'hit' or a 'miss'. Guest panel members in the 1960s included Cilla Black, Sid James, Brian Epstein, Freddie Garrity and Adam Faith. On 7 December 1963 the panel was made up of the four Beatles, and on 4 July 1964 it consisted of the five Rolling Stones. The original theme was *Juke Box Fury*, written and performed by Tony Osborne under the name of Ozzie Warlock and the Wizards, but the theme was changed in 1960 to the more familiar, *Hit and Miss*, by the John Barry Seven.

The Likely Lads (1964–66): BBC1. A situation comedy series created and written by Dick Clement and Ian La Frenais. It starred the perfectly cast duo of James Bolam and Rodney Bewes as Terry Collier and Bob Ferris. Set in the mid-1960s, it featured Terry and Bob as two working-class young men from Newcastle who had been best friends since childhood. The two characters were complete opposites: Terry was a hopeless, work-shy, but opinionated Jack-the-lad character, while Bob was a smartly dressed traditionalist man of reason. In the 1970s the two were reunited for the sequel, *Whatever Happened to the Likely Lads* (1973–74), which was filmed in colour.

The Lone Ranger (produced 1949–57; repeated through-out the 1960s): ITV. This was the best-known adaptation of the Lone Ranger story, the masked Texas Ranger hero who righted injustices in the American Old West with his trusty Indian sidekick, Tonto. It starred Clayton Moore as the Lone Ranger (except for a two-year period, between 1952–54, when Clayton Moore was in dispute and John Hart stood in) and Jay Silverheels as Tonto. 'Nowhere in the pages of history can one find a greater champion of justice.' At the end of each episode, one of the grateful subjects of his heroism would always ask, 'Who was that masked man?'

These two cowboy adventure series were show again and again on television throughout the 1960s (*The Lone Ranger* was actually made in the 1950s).

only to be told, 'Why, he's the Lone Ranger!' ... 'Hi-yo Silver, away!'

Magpie (1968–80): Thames Television for ITV. A children's television programme created by Lewis Judd in the style of the BBC's long-running *Blue Peter*, but presented in a trendier format. Its 1960s presenters were the former BBC Radio DJ Pete Brady, Susan Stranks, Tony Bastable and Douglas Rae.

The Man from U.N.C.L.E. (1964–68): BBC1. An American television secret agent series that followed the exploits of two secret agents, Napoleon Solo, played by Robert Vaughn, and Illya Kuryakin, played by David McCullum. Both worked for the United Network Command for Law and Enforcement whose headquarters were located behind a secret doorway in Del Floria's tailor shop on New York's East Side. The two heroes were involved in an endless fight against the agents of THRUSH (Technical Hierarchy for the Removal of Undesirables and the Subjugation of Humanity). Many well-known guests made an appearance, including William Shatner, Kurt Russell, Joan Collins, Nancy Sinatra, Sonny Bono and Cher, Joan Crawford and Telly Savalas.

Maverick (1957–62): ITV. An American western series that originally starred James Garner as the humorous and likeable Bret Maverick, a travelling poker player, and Jack Kelly as his equally keen card-playing brother, Bart Maverick. The stories revolved around the difficult situations their gambling got them into. Garner left the series in 1960 and was replaced by Roger Moore, who played cousin Beau Maverick. Garners' departure led to a slide in the show's popularity and Robert Colbert was brought in to play another brother, Brent Maverick. But the show was never as popular as it had

been with James Garner in the lead role, and so the series was dropped in 1962.

Mission Impossible (1966–73): ITV. American drama series that follows the exploits of the Impossible Missions Force (IMF), a small team of secret agents used for covert missions against evil organisations. The identities of the organisation that oversaw the IMF and the government it worked for were never revealed. Each week, secret agent Jim Phelps (Peter Graves) would receive instructions for a new mission, 'Your mission, Jim, should you accept it …' Each agent had his or her own special talent that would be used to help the team succeed in the impossible mission.

The Monkees (1966–68): ITV. An American comedy/pop music show that followed a pop group's (the Monkees) madcap adventures. The four members of the group were brought together specially for this show, having been selected from 400 applicants. It starred Mickey Dolenz, Michael Nesmith, Peter Tork and British actor Davy Jones as the Monkees. As a pop group, the Monkees had seven UK top-twenty hit records, including *I'm a Believer*, which went to number one in the UK charts in January 1967.

Morecambe and Wise (*Two of a Kind*: 1961–68, ATV for ITV; *The Morecambe and Wise Show*: 1968–77, BBC): It was in the 1960s shows that we first heard those popular catch-phrases: 'I'll smash your face in', 'Get out of that' and 'More tea Ern?' Eric Morecambe and Ernie Wise were the funniest comedy duo on television in the sixties. All the top celebrities queued up to be on the show and to be jokingly told by Eric that they were 'Rubbish!' The long list of guests included The Beatles, the Kinks, Engelbert Humperdinck, Matt Monro and Bruce Forsyth.

The Newcomers (1965–69): BBC1. A twice-weekly half-hour soap opera about a London family, the Coopers, who moved into a new housing estate in the fictional English country town of Angleton. The cast included Alan Browning, Judy Geeson and Wendy Richard.

No Hiding Place (1959–67): Associated-Rediffusion for ITV. A British crime series which followed the cases of Detective Superintendent Tom Lockhart (Raymond Francis) of Scotland Yard.

Opportunity Knocks (1964–78): ABC, then Thames Television for ITV. A British television talent show hosted by Hughie Green. A studio 'clapometer' measured the studio audience's opinion of each act, but this didn't count towards the final result. The winning act was decided by postal votes sent in by the viewing public and the winner was announced the following week. Les Dawson (1967) and Mary Hopkin (1968) were among the 1960s contestants who went on to become famous. The BBC later revived the show (1987–90).

Perry Mason (1957–66): BBC TV and BBC1. This American legal drama series starred Raymond Burr as a fictional Los Angeles defence attorney, Perry Mason, who always won his cases. Perry would solve the cases with the help of his investigator, Paul Drake, played by William Hopper, and his confidential secretary, Della Street, played by Barbara Hale. They did it all by themselves, sometimes they even found the body! And of course the police and the district attorney always charged the wrong person with the crime. The programme would end with Perry Mason getting the real villain to break down in the courtroom's witness box and admit to having done it.

The Phil Silvers Show (1955–59, re-run in the 1960s): Phil Silvers played the fast-talking Sergeant Ernie Bilko in this American situation comedy, in which he and his subordinate team of soldiers undertook all sorts of get-rich-quick schemes behind the back of Colonel John T. Hall, played by Paul Ford, at the fictional Fort Baxter. Other cast members included Harvey Lembeck as Corporal Rocco Barbella, Allan Melvin as Corporal Steve Henshaw, Herbie Faye as Private Sam Fender and Maurice Gosfield as the slovenly Private Duane Doberman.

Please Sir! (1968–72): LWT for ITV. A situation comedy series set in the fictional Fenn Street School, with teacher, Bernard Hedges (John Alderton), doing his best to control the rowdy but likeable students of class 5C. The cast included Derek Guyler as Norman Potter the caretaker, Joan Sanderson as fearsome teacher Doris Ewell, and Richard Davis as Welsh teacher Mr Price. The class of 5C pupils included smooth-talking Peter Craven (Malcolm McFee), wise-cracking Eric Duffy (Peter Cleall), dim-witted Dennis Dunstable (Peter Denver), mummy's boy and wannabe tough guy Frankie Abbott (David Barry), sexy Sharon Eversleigh (Penny Spencer) and soppy Maureen Bullock (Liz Gebhardt) who was hopelessly in love with Mr Hedges.

Popeye the Sailor (1960–62 and re-run thereafter): ITV. The cartoon adventures of Popeye the sailor man, his girl-friend Olive Oyl and his love rival, the villainous brute Bluto. There was also the infant, Swee' Pea, who was found abandoned, and the hamburger-munching J. Wellington Wimpy. The adventures always involved a punch-up with Bluto, with Popeye eventually winning after gaining some

extra muscular strength by swallowing a can of spinach. This show was a firm favourite with the kids and was repeated throughout the 1960s.

The Prisoner (1967–68): ITC for ITV. A cult television drama series that nobody seemed to understand, but everyone kept watching anyway. It starred the show's co-creator Patrick McGoohan who, after resigning as a British secret agent, is kidnapped and taken to an unnamed village in an unknown location, where he is to be known only as 'Number Six'. The village authorities subject him to a series of psychological challenges designed to break his will and get inside his mind. The bizarre plots and the use of psychedelic imagery and nursery rhymes made this quite a weird drama series.

Ready Steady Go! (1963–66): Associated-Rediffusion for ITV. It was a very popular rock/pop music television show presented by Keith Fordyce and Cathy McGowan, who was dubbed 'Queen of the Mods'. The programme usually started with the slogan, 'The Weekend Starts Here'. The show included interviews, chat, fashion, competitions and the latest pop music. The audience and dancers were also allowed to mingle with the guest artists on the studio floor. Initially, guest artists mimed to records, but from 1964 some were performing live, and by April 1965 all performances were live. The show featured the most successful artists of the era, including The Beatles, Dusty Springfield (who sometimes also presented it), the Supremes, the Rolling Stones, The Who, the Dave Clark Five, the Beach Boys and the Small Faces.

The Rolf Harris Show (1967–70): BBC1. A popular light entertainment show featuring Rolf Harris and his guests.

On Friday 2 April 1965, the popular television rock/pop music programme, *Ready Steady Go!* went live for the first time, which meant that artists appearing on the show had to perform live instead of miming. The picture is of Cathy McGowan, the show's presenter.

On each show Rolf would paint wonderful pictures on a huge whiteboard – 'Can you tell what it is yet?' Not forgetting Rolf's trademark wobbleboard and didgeridoo, both of which he often used as accompanying instruments when he sang.

Rowan and Martin's Laugh-In (1968–73): BBC2. An American comedy sketch show hosted by comedians Dan Rowan and Dick Martin with a bewildering array of guests. The show was filled with a series of quick-fire gags and sketches involving familiar regular guests that included Ruth Buzzi, Judy Carne, Henry Gibson, Goldie Hawn, Arthur 'Arte' Johnson, Jo Anne Worley and Alan Sues.

The Saint (1962–69): ITC for ITV. A mystery spy thriller series, starring Roger Moore as Simon Templar, The Saint, who was billed as the Robin Hood of modern crime. The fictional detective was created by Leslie Charteris and featured in many of his novels. The television series portrayed the London-based Simon Templar as a secret agent who solved all sorts of mysteries in fantasy-style plots. In 1978, the series was revived as *Return of the Saint*, starring Ian Ogilvy as Simon Templar.

Softly, Softly (1966–69): BBC1. A British drama series centred on the work of a regional crime squad based in the fictional area of Wyvern, somewhere in England. The programme was a spin-off from the popular *Z-Cars* series after the original series ended in 1965. As with the *Z-Cars* series, *Softly, Softly* featured Detective Chief Inspector Charles Barlow and Detective Inspector John Watt, played by Stratford Johns and Frank Windsor.

Star Trek (1969–71): BBC1. This was the first series of Star Trek programmes. They aired in America from 1966–69,

Steptoe and Son, the fictional father and son rag-and-bone men from Shepherd's Bush, first appeared on our television screens in 1962. From the left, the picture shows Harold Steptoe (played by Harry H. Corbett), Hercules the horse and Albert Steptoe (played by Wilfred Brambell).

but didn't make it to the UK until July 1969. These episodes starred William Shatner as Captain James T. Kirk, Leonard Nimoy as Commander Spock, DeForest Kelley as Lt Commander Leonard 'Bones' McCoy, James Doohan as Montgomery 'Scotty' Scott, Nichelle Nichols as Nyota Uhura, George Takei as Hikaru Sulu, Walter Koenig as Pavel Chekov, Grace Lee Whitney as Janice Rand and Majel Barrett as Christine Chapel. They all voyaged on the starship Enterprise's 'five-year mission to explore strange new worlds, to seek out new life and new civilizations, to boldly go where no man has gone before'.

Steptoe and Son (1962–65 & 1970–74): BBC TV, then BBC1. A British situation comedy written by Ray Galton and Alan Simpson about the lives of two fictional rag-and-bone men living in the fictional Oil Drum Lane in Shepherd's Bush, London. The long-running series was born out of a one-off *Comedy Playhouse* play called *The Offer*. In a 2004 poll done by the BBC, the show was voted fifteenth best British sitcom of all time.

Sunday Night at the London Palladium (1955–67): ATV for ITV. A British television variety show produced by Val Parnell. The regular 1960s hosts were Bruce Forsyth (1958–60 and 1961), Don Arrol (1960–61), Norman Vaughan (1962–65) and Jimmy Tarbuck (1965–67). Entertainment included the Tiller Girls, speciality acts and top artists of the time. The middle of the show featured the popular game show, *Beat the Clock*, in which members of the audience were invited to complete unusual tasks in a short period of time, measured by a large clock at the back of the stage. The show ended each week with all the guests assembled on a revolving stage. The show was briefly revived in 1973 and 1974.

Thank Your Lucky Stars was a weekly British television pop music show made by ABC television for ITV from 1961–66. It featured many of the top bands and artists of the day.

Take Your Pick (1955–68): ITV. A popular quiz show in which quizmaster, Michael Miles, invited contestants to answer simple questions for 60 seconds without them using the words 'yes' or 'no'. Alec Dane stood next to him with a gong, ready to sound it at the contestant if they uttered the forbidden words. If the contestant got through that round then they could select any key from one of thirteen boxes. Miles would offer them increasing amounts of money in exchange for the key. If the money didn't tempt the contestant then he or she went on to open their chosen box. Three of the boxes would contain booby prizes and box thirteen would contain a mystery prize. There was also a 'treasure chest of money' and 'tonight's star prize', which was always a three-piece-suite – 'O-o-o-o-o-o-h-h!'

That Was The Week That Was (aka *TW3*) (1962–63): BBC TV. A groundbreaking satirical television comedy programme that was devised, produced and directed by Ned Sherrin and presented by David Frost. No target was deemed to be out of bounds and nothing and nobody was spared criticism, from royalty and religion to politicians and businessmen. For the first time on British television, they were all made fun of by cast members that included Bernard Levin, Lance Percival, Kenneth Cope, Roy Kinnear, Willie Rushden, Frankie Howerd and Millicent Martin. The show had a huge team of off-screen scriptwriters that included John Bird, Graham Chapman, John Cleese, Peter Cook, Frank Muir, Denis Norden, Bill Oddie and Eric Sykes (to name but a few).

Thank Your Lucky Stars (1961–66): ABC for ITV. A British pop music television show that featured many of the top artists and bands of the era. The show's hosts included Jim

Dale, Pete Murray and Keith Fordyce, but the main host throughout the series was Brian Matthews. The girl with the strong Black Country accent, Janice 'Oi'll give it foive' Nicholls, joined the show in 1963 as part of a team that reviewed new records.

Thunderbirds (1965–66): ATV for ITV. A British television marionette puppet show devised by Gerry and Sylvia Anderson and made by A.P. Films. The series followed the adventures of the Tracy family, who ran International Rescue, an organisation created to help those in grave danger using technically advanced equipment. They flew on rescue missions in their futuristic space and aqua vehicles called Thunderbirds. The team consisted of Jeff Tracy (ex-astronaut and head of the organisation), Scott (pilot of reconnaissance rocket Thunderbird 1), Virgil (pilot of vehicle transporter Thunderbird 2), Alan (astronaut of space rocket Thunderbird 3), Gordon (aquanaut of submarine Thunderbird 4), John (operator of space station Thunderbird 5), Brains (scientist), Lady Penelope (the London agent) and Parker (Lady Penelope's chauffeur). And let's not forget Lady Penelope's pink Rolls-Royce car, FAB 1.

Till Death Us Do Part (1965–75): BBC1. A British situation comedy series created by Johnny Speight and starring Warren Mitchell as Alf Garnett, the head of a fictional working-class family in London's East End. Each week, Alf subjected his wife, daughter, son-in-law, and anyone else who would listen, to bigoted rants about everything from immigration to the permissive society. He referred to his long-suffering wife Else (Dandy Nichols) as a 'silly moo', and his work-shy Liverpudlian son-in-law, Mike Rawlins (Anthony Booth), as a 'Scouse git'. Una Stubbs played

There was an abundance of children's comics and magazines around in the 1960s, including these two from the television series *Thunderbirds*; *Lady Penelope* for girls and *Thunderbirds* for boys, *c.* 1966.

Alf's daughter, Rita. The series attracted a lot of complaints; one of its main critics being Mary Whitehouse, the self-appointed moral guardian of the sixties. The offensive language used by Alf Garnet's character especially outraged her: 'I doubt if many people would use 121 bloodies in half an hour.'

Top of the Pops (1964–2006): BBC1. A half-hour pop music UK-chart television programme broadcast every Thursday evening at 7.30 p.m. The first ever show was on New Year's Day 1964 and was presented by the then 37-year-old disc jockey, Jimmy Savile. The Rolling Stones were the first artists to appear on that first show, miming to their latest hit, *I Wanna Be Your Man* (written by Lennon & McCartney). Other artists that appeared on the show were Dusty Springfield, the Dave Clark Five, the Hollies and the Swinging Blue Jeans. Pre-filmed clips were also shown of Cliff Richard and the Shadows, Freddie and the Dreamers and The Beatles, who played the week's number one, *I Want To Hold Your Hand*. For the first two years, the presenters were Jimmy Savile, Alan Freeman, Pete Murray and David Jacobs, who each took turns. There was also the regular 'disc-girl' presenter, Samantha Juste. Other 1960s presenters (1966–70) included Simon Dee and Tony Blackburn. Initially, artists mimed to their records, but in July 1966 miming was banned. That only lasted for a few weeks because some artists' live performances were found to be of poor quality, and so specially recorded backing-tracks were permitted in order to produce a good 'live sound'.

Wagon Train (1958–64): ITV. Very popular hour-long western series starring Ward Bond as wagon master Major Seth Adams and Robert Horton as Flint McCullough.

You will probably also remember old Charlie Wooster, the comical cook, played by Frank McGrath. Each week, the wagon train team managed to save some pioneering settlers from the Indians as they made their way through the endless deserts and Rocky Mountain passes in covered wagons. Lots of exciting horseback chases and loads of guest stars.

Watch with Mother (1952–73): BBC TV and BBC1. Created by Freda Lingstrom as television's answer to radio's *Listen with Mother*. Originally known as *For the Children*, which had been on television since before the war and first introduced us to *Muffin the Mule* in 1946, *Watch with Mother* brought together a daily sequence of programmes aimed at pre-school children, including *Picture Book, Andy Pandy, The Flowerpot Men, Rag, Tag and Bobtail, The Woodentops* and *Camberwick Green.*

The Worker (1965 and 1969–70): ATV for ITV. A comedy series starring Charlie Drake as 'The Worker', a hopeless unemployed labourer who is sent to a new job in every episode by Mr Pugh (played by Henry McGee), the Labour Exchange clerk. But Charlie never lasted more than a day before being sacked and having to return to the Labour Exchange, and the exasperated Mr Pugh.

The Val Doonican Show (1965–86): BBC1. This variety entertainment show featured Val Doonican singing songs and introducing guest artists. Who could ever forget his trademark woollen jumpers, rocking chair and acoustic guitar? And there were all those comical Irish songs, like *Paddy McGinty's Goat, Delaney's Donkey* and *O'Rafferty's Motor Car.* Doonican was a very popular entertainer and achieved five UK top-ten hit singles in the 1960s: *Walk Tall* (1964), *The Special Years* (1965), *Elusive Butterfly* (1966),

What Would I Be (1966) and *If the Whole World Stopped Loving Me* (1967).

The Virginian (1962–70): BBC TV and BBC1. A 90-minute weekly television western series featuring 'The Virginian' (his real name was never revealed), played by James Drury, who was a foreman on the fictional Shiloh Ranch in Medicine Bow, Wyoming. It also starred Doug McClure who played the Virginian's side-kick, Trampas. Many famous stars appeared as guests in the series, including Charles Bronson, Joan Crawford, Harrison Ford, Lee Marvin, Leslie Nielsen, Robert Redford and William Shatner.

Z-Cars (1962–65 & 1967–78): BBC TV and BBC1. A British television police drama series centred on the fictional town of Newtown, Liverpool. The stories revolved around the activities of pairs of police officers patrolling the local streets. The main characters included DCI Charlie Barlow (Stratford Johns), DS John Watt (Frank Windsor), PC 'Fancy' Smith (Brian Blessed), PC 'Jock' Weir (Joseph Brady) and PC Bert Lynch (James Ellis).

Zoo Time (1956–68): ITV. Featured Desmond Morris, with the help of various animal experts and zoo staff from Regent's Park Zoo in London. Lots of information about animals, using pictures taken from around the zoo. The early shows always featured Congo, the chimpanzee, who learned how to draw and paint.

Eight

SCHOOLDAYS AND HOLIDAYS

When you were a child, the classroom in your infants school seemed huge, but in reality it was just an average-sized room filled with lots of very small desks. It used to take you absolutely ages to run from one side of the school playground to the other, but now you can walk its full length in a matter of seconds. It's so hard to believe that you were ever that small. Mind you, in the 1960s, kids were smaller than children of a similar age today. Even so, until recently, school furniture was still being made to roughly the same size as it was then, resulting in many of today's kids having to squeeze into ill-fitting desks and chairs. But, even though the size of the furniture wasn't an issue in the 1960s, the chairs were just as hard and so you did have a good excuse for all that fidgeting.

It's amazing how much you learnt in those seven young years at primary school. Looking back, many people can attribute a great deal of what they learnt to the efforts of just one teacher. As in every generation, teachers had varying levels of knowledge and teaching skills. Some were lazy and boring, limiting themselves to teaching the basic three 'Rs', whereas others were true vocational teachers that involved themselves in every aspect of teaching; attending after-school courses to learn additional subjects like drama, painting, crafts and music. These were more often than not the inspirational teachers that made everything interesting and could enthuse you to learn. If you were lucky enough to have had one of those enterprising primary school teachers then you will appreciate the contribution that he or she made to your childhood development.

Such teachers had the ability to provide a complete mix of education and to make schoolwork enjoyable. It was usually the same resourceful teacher that taught you how to read, write and do sums who then took you off to the local baths for swimming lessons, arranged needlework and dance classes for the girls and showed them how to play netball, and still found time to teach the boys how to play football and cricket properly. He or she would have been there when you were given your first tambourine, triangle or recorder to play as part of the enthusiastic but shambolic school orchestra. It was that same teacher who made sure that you were word perfect in the school play, organised the school choir and taught you all of those now familiar carols that you sang at the school's Christmas carol concerts – proving that it really was possible for you to sing and breathe at the same time.

On cold winter days, your teacher sat at the front of the class and bewitched you with readings from children's fictional storybooks, or fascinated you with tales of British history; the ancient Egyptian mummies, the Battle of Hastings in 1066, King John and the Magna Carta of 1215. It made you feel warm inside and even though playtime was fast approaching you didn't want the story to end.

Your teacher took you on nature walks and taught you how to look after Joey the hamster; showed you how to mould plasticine and cover the moulding with gooey strips of newspaper to make papier mâché models. You were also taught a variety of crafts, from painting pictures and murals to making collages, and even basket weaving. In summer, your teacher would have been there on the school sports day to help prepare you for the sack race, the egg and spoon and wheelbarrow races; in winter, he or she would have been there to encourage you on those awful muddy cross-country runs.

Why was it that you were always dragged out on the coldest and wettest winter's day to do a cross-country run? And it always seemed to be cold and wet on the days you went to the swimming baths as well. Everyone was always shivering in those poolside changing huts, or cupboards more like!

At Christmas time, having decorated the classroom and organised the school Christmas party, where you were taught how to play party games like pass the parcel, musical chairs and blind man's buff, it was your class teacher who would bring in some of the latest pop records from home for you to sing and dance to.

A selection from the 1960s Ladybird *Key Words* series of books for young children.

Did you think I would leave you crying

When there's room on my horse for two

Climb up here Jack and don't be crying

I can go just as fast with two

When we grow up we'll both be soldiers

And our horses will not be toys

And I wonder if we'll remember

When we were two little boys.

(Words by Edward Madden, 1902)

Rolf Harris's version of *Two Little Boys* reached number one in the UK record charts in November 1969.

From playing with small beanbags in the school hall to your first game of rounders in the playground, and even dressing up for a part in the Christmas nativity play, your primary school teacher showed you how to do it all – And still managed to teach you 'the three Rs'!

You will surely still have many memories of your time at primary school; remember queuing up in just your vest and pants to see the school doctor and the nit nurse? The playtime bell, the school tuck shop, the five-bob a week school dinner money, free school milk in those strange third-of-a-pint glass bottles, girls swapping beads they kept in tobacco tins and boys swapping cigarette cards; girls in miniskirts having dancing lessons and boys in tight-fitting shorts playing five-a-side football; the smell of coal dust in the school boiler room, looking at an eclipse of the sun through a photographic negative, walking home on dark winter evenings and struggling to get to school during the big freeze of 1963. And then there was the storeroom where

the school caretaker kept all the old broken desks and chairs – why were they never thrown out?

Eleven-Plus Exam

Everything you learned at primary school was in preparation for the eleven-plus exams, which you took soon after your eleventh birthday. You were used to being given a set of sums to calculate, or a composition to write for English, but you had never before experienced such an examination. Your parents and teachers drummed into you the importance of the exam, and everyone got very nervous about it. The original purpose of the eleven-plus exam was for the authorities to use the results to place children into secondary schools that best suited their abilities, so their talents could be suitably developed for use in their future careers. Unfortunately, however well-intended the original plans were, the results of the eleven-plus examinations simply became a matter of passing or failing. This was a life-changing event for which you had sole responsibility, and sadly, the result could only go one of two ways – 'pass' and you were an academic success and going on to grammar school, or 'fail' and you were going to a secondary modern with every chance of leaving school at the age of 15 with little or no qualifications, unless you went on to college. Many kids had no real understanding of what the differences were between grammar and secondary modern schools. They were happy if they could go to the same school as their classmates and older siblings, preferably near to where they lived.

On the morning of the exam, there was an air of importance and secrecy that you had never known before. You were told not to talk to anyone, pass messages or to look around at all until the examinations were over. That bit was easy because such restrictions were just part of the standard rules in any 1960s classroom, particularly when you did tests. However, you had never previously been given such a comprehensive test, and it had never before been so important for you to write neatly and get the answers right. The question papers were placed upside down on your desk in front of you and at the appointed hour, when the papers had all been distributed, you were told to turn them over and begin.

The exam was in three parts: arithmetic and problem solving, general English (including comprehension and an essay) and general knowledge. In the later 1960s, in an attempt to make the exam fairer, more emphasis was put on general knowledge questions. Try these two early eleven-plus exam questions:

Q1. Subtract two-thirds of 834 from 23 times 185.

Q2. Seven piles of bricks are placed side by side so that their tops form steps one brick high. If the lowest pile contains nine bricks, how many bricks are being used altogether?

Remember this was for 11-year-olds, there were no calculators and you had to show all your workings-out on the paper, including crossings-out. It was before decimalisation and so questions to do with money were shown and calculated in the old pounds, shillings and pence (£ s d),

and children were mainly taught to use fractions rather than decimals when doing calculations.

A1. 3,699

A2. 84 bricks

Whether through exam nerves, borderline test results or something else, there is no doubt that failure was not restricted to the less brainy candidates. Many clever kids also failed the eleven-plus exam and found themselves shipped into what were often poor performing secondary modern schools. Such children seeking an academic future then frequently found that they had a mountain to climb in order to achieve their ambitions.

Once the emotions of results day had calmed down, there was then the overwhelming realisation that friends were going to be split up and sent to different schools. Some that lived a distance apart might never see each other again. It broke up many long-term friendships, and in working-class areas the grammar school kids would often find themselves ostracised and branded as snobs by their old mates, who believed that they no longer had anything in common. Passing the eleven-plus did not in itself guarantee entry to secondary school, as all grammar schools and some secondary modern schools required applicants to attend selection interviews from which the school would pick the best of the bunch. The school interview was the second biggest life-changing occurrence in your young life over which you had influence. It would determine whether or not you were to go to your school of choice.

School Friend was just one of the many schoolgirl annuals that would be regularly swapped between schoolmates.

Secondary School

Whatever school you ended up in, you then had to come to terms with being one of the new kids – what a turn of events! After all, you had come from the comfortable and familiar surroundings of your primary school, which, after some seven years, had earned you position and respect as one of the 'top dogs' in the playground, and all of a sudden you find yourself relegated to the bottom of a new ladder, being among the smallest, weakest and dumbest in this strange and unfamiliar place. The whole ethos was different. You were now surrounded by huge spotty youths with attitude, whose main occupation during break times was to stand around in groups talking. Not only did you need to learn and adjust to the new school's rules, but you also had to quickly familiarise yourself with the unwritten rules of the playground, such as the unmarked areas that, over time, had become reserved territory for certain groups of older students. There was also a pecking order for inheriting a particular area of playground when its previous occupiers were promoted to a better patch or left the school altogether. There was even a league for 'best patch in the playground', often where there was something to lean against, like a fence or a wall, and preferably out of sight of any teachers monitoring the playground. Many older schools still had outside toilet blocks and these were often used as hideaways for smokers rather than for their proper purpose. Teachers and prefects would regularly raid the toilet blocks to catch pupils smoking, and so innocent non-smokers would avoid going there in case they were wrongly caught up in a 'smokers raid'. Unfortunately,

judgements were often swift and there was no appeal – if in doubt, guilty! As a new and young first former, you were seen as an obvious target for general bullying and there were the usual initiation ceremonies to endure, like pushing your head down the toilet pan and flushing the cistern, and making you stand on a piping hot radiator in bare feet. Of course, not every school was like that; many kids went right through their schooldays and never came across any form of physical punishment or bullying. Every school was different, but the way that each school was run didn't necessarily relate to how rough a school was; many of the best academic schools had some of the strictest rules and the harshest teachers. Whatever welcome you got at your new secondary school, you will have experienced an anxious settling-in period, but within days you would have regained your confidence and begun to feel much older and more distant from your primary school days. The childish games of old were soon erased from your mind as you adjusted to learning mathematics instead of 'sums', foreign languages and all those new specialist subjects like physics, chemistry, economics and Latin. There was an awful lot to take in, and some even had to deal with the disappointment of being placed in a single-sex school. And then there was all the homework!

The method of learning was so different back then – everything came out of books. This was at a time when the word 'computer' wasn't yet used in everyday language and even commercial computers, which were the size of a room, were quite new. Knowledge was gathered from schoolbooks and library reference books. There was no such thing as 'copy and paste' from web pages downloaded from

Enid Blyton's *St Clare's* series of books was always popular reading for young girls.

the Internet. Even handheld pocket calculators hadn't yet been invented, and all mathematical calculations were done using pen and paper with just the aid of your brain. From a very young age you were taught your times tables and were constantly tested on your ability to recite them and answer on-the-spot questions. Maths teachers would randomly point at individuals around the class and fire questions at them – Nine eights? Twelve sevens? Eleven fours?

At school you did loads of physical education and sports, with hard-working PE sessions two or three days a week, and typically there would be a weekly games afternoon for competition sports like football, rugby, cricket, rounders, tennis, hockey, netball and athletics. There was also extra training after school, and school league competitions were held on Saturdays. Just to be sure that you used up every spare ounce of energy, some schools even taught and competed in additional sports like boxing, judo and weight-lifting.

Everything was so different at secondary school; with your new friends and a much heavier workload, you just didn't have time to look back at your primary school days. You were gradually leaving your childhood behind and moving ever closer to becoming a moody teenager.

School Uniform

Most kids growing up in the ultra trendy sixties hated having to wear a school uniform. It was considered very 'uncool' to be seen wearing your uniform outside school. It was even worse for those with brightly coloured blaz-

ers and embarrassing hats. This was the first generation of pre-teenage schoolchildren to get bitten by the fashion bug, wanting to be as trendy as only older teenagers had been before. Young boys and girls began ditching their old traditional leather satchels in favour of large holdall bags, big enough for them to stuff their blazer and tie into as soon as they were far enough away from the school gates. Kids that had a long journey home would even pull on a fashionable casual top to cover up their regulation school shirt or blouse – anything to make them look more stylish and older than they really were. But even the super-cool action of puffing on a cigarette didn't convince anyone; the regulation 'fish box' school shoes were always a dead giveaway. With all the other stuff that was crammed into their school bags, there was barely enough room left to accommodate the latest *New Musical Express* newspaper, let alone a huge pair of 'fish box' shoes. Then there was the risk of getting caught travelling home without proper school uniform, which could mean a severe punishment at school the next day and the possibility of a letter being sent to your parents.

School Photo

Why was it that so many individual school photos looked so awful? Why were they always taken when your hair looked at its worse, all greasy and matted, and on the very day that an enormous red carbuncle had sprouted from the side of your nose? And why didn't they tell you that the knot of your school tie had slipped sideways and was halfway under your collar? To make matters worse, for the first

time ever, the school had arranged for the photographs to be taken using Kodachrome colour film, and so you would get a brilliantly clear colour image of the mountainous range of red spots and yellow heads emblazoned across your forehead. And your proud mum has already said that she wants a large size print to go in a frame on the mantelpiece! As well as the individual school photos, many secondary schools had a professional photograph taken of the whole school each year using a rotating panoramic camera that slowly panned around the assembled group of students and teachers. There were always stories of someone posing for the photograph at one end and then running around the back to get into the photo again at the other end, but many such claims were myths. Although someone would always say they were going to do it, or brag that they had done it, there was rarely any evidence of it actually being done. With the long group photograph, even though you were tightly wedged between hundreds of other students and you occupied a very small part of the overall picture, you were still convinced that your spotty forehead would shine out like a beacon.

Discipline

There was a firm code of discipline in all schools, but each school was left to decide what type of punishment would be given to a child that broke any of its rules. This meant that there was an enormous disparity in the severity of punishments dished out at different schools, particularly for boys. At some schools, a boy might be made to pick up

litter in the playground as a punishment for poor school-work or wrongdoing, but many preferred to use physical punishment, which was still legal back then. There was unlikely to be any litter in the playground at any all-boys school where physical punishment was practised because the boys wouldn't dare create it in the first place, for fear of a caning.

In primary schools, it was quite common for a teacher to slap a child across the back of the legs or hit them on the hand with a wooden ruler for misbehaving. The cane, slipper or tawse (in Scotland) was used in primary schools, but they were usually reserved for the older boys. You did hear stories of girls being caned or slapped with a slipper, but most beatings (corporal punishment) were inflicted on boys of secondary school age, and while the fear of a caning did keep unruly boys in check, a number of cruel and cowardly teachers undeniably relished the task of inflicting pain on small boys. Some all-boys secondary schools, particularly grammar and public schools, had a designated 'punishment room' where boys would be sent to be caned at lunch-times or after school, and in typically British fashion, boys would form an orderly queue outside the door to wait their turn. The head or deputy head teacher would sometimes perform the wicked deed, but quite often another more willing teacher would be given the task and put in charge of the 'punishment room'. Surprisingly, the authorities never questioned the motives of these eager participants, but the boys did. Schools were supposed to keep records of any corporal punishment they dished out in what were called 'punishment books', but the rule was not adhered to because punishments would often be meted out on the spur

of the moment in the classroom, and sometimes at random, with the teacher not knowing who was being beaten, or even losing count of the number of strokes being landed on target. Clouts across the back of the head for not paying attention were commonplace and there was an unending supply of chalk, blackboard dusters and other missiles thrown across the classroom as instant recognition of someone's misbehaviour.

It was not uncommon for boys to be ceremonially caned in front of the class and sometimes in front of the whole school. This was usually done for bringing the school into disrepute, fighting in the street while in school uniform or barging in front of an old lady at a local bus stop. Apart from corporal punishment, other forms of chastisement included after-school detention, writing lines 'I must not ...' and running around the perimeter of the playground or playing field. Whatever the punishment, there was an unwritten rule that discouraged boys from telling their parents when they had been punished at school. It was also unwise to tell them because you were likely to get another whack from them for having misbehaved at school in the first place, and you were obviously guilty! The absolute worst humiliation was for a parent to come to the school and complain. There was nothing worse than to have your mum turn up at the school to fight your battles for you.

The antics of fictional cane-wielding headmaster Prof. James Edwards MA, as portrayed by Jimmy Edwards in the early sixties television comedy series *Whack-O!* were not entirely imaginary, and Professor Edwards' favourite saying, 'Bend over, Wendover!', was true to life for many a 1960s schoolboy.

Holidays

Throughout the school year, children would dream of their six-week summer holiday break and of what they would do and where they would go. By the mid-sixties, an increasing number of working-class families were abandoning the traditional British bucket-and-spade seaside holidays in favour of the newly arrived, and now affordable, package foreign holidays. For the first time, ordinary kids were being taken to exciting European cities and holiday resorts that they had previously only seen pictured in glossy magazines. People brought back all sorts of souvenirs to remind them of the places they had visited and the different cultures they had experienced. There was now a pair of wooden castanets hanging from the hook on the back of the bedroom door where you once proudly hung a kiss-me-quick hat that you got while holidaying in Bognor Regis. Your personalised Spanish Matador poster is stuck firmly to the bedroom wall and is now your second favourite poster of all time, only just losing out to the picture of a stunning red E-Type Jaguar that is in pride of place above your bed. In the living room, the sideboard is littered with all sorts of tacky souvenir ornaments, including ones of the Leaning Tower of Pisa and the Eiffel Tower. Goodbye to Margate – Benidorm here we come. Oh, to have experienced such new holiday delights!

Meanwhile, back home in Britain, the likes of Butlins, Pontins and Warners continued to excite holidaymakers with all the usual join-in-and-be-jolly holiday camp stuff. And caravan and camping sites all over the country were still bursting at the seams with summer visitors, as were

Typical family camping holiday at Billing Aquadrome Holiday Park in Northampton, *c.* 1964.

Children's donkey rides at Burnham-on-Sea, Somerset, *c.* 1965.

the traditional seaside boarding houses. In the 1960s, many working adults still only got two weeks paid holiday a year, with part-timers and piece-workers getting no holiday pay at all. They often had to take their holiday at a time determined by their employer, usually during the factory's summer closedown period in August. And they needed to have the cash available to go on holiday because nobody in Britain had a credit card until 1966, when Barclaycard launched the first one, and many people didn't even have a bank account. It was several years later before the use of credit cards became commonplace in this country (the second credit card, Access, was only launched in 1972). In spite of the increasing popularity of foreign package holidays, the traditional British bucket-and-spade seaside holiday was still alive and well throughout the sixties, with the penny arcades, Punch and Judy shows, paddling pools

and funfair rides still providing plenty of amusement for the kids. And all of the typical British seafront specials were still proving to be popular with British holidaymakers, from candyfloss and peppermint rock to jellied eels and whelks, and not forgetting the saucy picture postcards. You just couldn't get that sort of thing on a fancy foreign holiday in Majorca.

Whether you holidayed at home or abroad, in the sixties many people were still ignorant of the dangers from too much unprotected exposure to the sun's ultraviolet radiation, and many annual visitors to the seaside would stay on the beach all day without using any suncream at all, their skin slowly burning under the sun's rays to a glowing red lobster-like colour, and in the evening there was the ritual of slapping on loads of calamine lotion to calm the sore sunburned skin. Lots of boys believed that suncream was just for girls and wimps, and many girls used it sparingly because they thought it hindered their bid for a quick suntan. After all, it was important not to arrive back home from holiday looking all pale and white skinned, as though you hadn't been to the seaside at all. In the evening, if you weren't confined to bed with sunstroke, you would put on something white to show off your newly acquired crimson tan; your burning skin radiating heat into the cool night air, even though you actually felt quite shivery. The real problems began in bed that night, by which time the full effects of the day's sun had taken its toll and you couldn't bear the weight or even the touch of a single pink calamine powder-stained sheet on the tight skin of your burning shoulders and back. You lay motionless on your front, hoping that the exhaustion you felt from the day's adventures would force

you into a deep sleep and make you oblivious to the horrible stinging pain and feverishness that you now felt. The next morning, you looked in the mirror to see patches of peeling skin hanging from your shoulders, and further examination revealed evidence that lots more loose skin was beginning to lift from other parts of your body. All proof that the hard-earned instant suntan was just peeling away before your very eyes, but, undeterred, you prayed for another sunny day to come.

Nine

CHRISTMAS

Christmas is always the most special time of year for children, and it was no different in the 1960s. Christmas was much less commercialised than it is today and the overall preparation started much later. At school, there was always the usual exciting build-up to the big day with the making of Christmas decorations and decorating the classroom. Then there was the school nativity play and the carol concerts, which made the celebrations all-inclusive, even for non-Christians. At home, a sure sign of Christmas approaching was when your mum started to knit a 'lovely' Christmas jumper for some lucky recipient. Knitting was still very popular then with women and girls of all ages. You had experienced only a small number of Christmases so far in your short young life and it was still all so excit-

An ABC theatre programme for the Blackpool Holiday Startime Season 1966, featuring Cilla Black and the Bachelors.

ing for you. Each year, there was something new to interest and excite you, and as you got older you were allowed to help more with the preparations: writing Christmas cards, making a crib to go on the sideboard, blowing up balloons and putting up decorations in the living room. It was such a huge annual event that completely brightened up an otherwise cold and horrible winter. The Christmas tree was always the crowning glory, usually put up and decorated on Christmas Eve with the customary angel or fairy doll perched at the very top. Whatever you called it, angel or fairy, the same pretty winged doll would be used. There were baubles, bells, ribbons and fairy lights; chocolate coins wrapped in gold foil and balls of cotton wool for snow. Then there were the sprigs of holly and mistletoe to hang from the ceiling; it was all so wonderfully exciting.

Christmas Shopping

The big department stores were magical places to visit at Christmas time, with huge window displays depicting all sorts of wonderful Christmas scenes. Inside, all of the stores would have enormous Christmas trees and brightly coloured decorations throughout. There was always a strong smell of perfume and leather permeating the ground floor areas. Each store had vast ranges of toys and presents on display, and they would all try to outdo each other in trying to build the most welcoming and realistic Santa's Grotto. It was in the days when children were still encouraged to sit on Santa's knee and tell him what they wanted for Christmas. The experience terrified and confused kids;

it contradicted everything they had ever been taught about being cautious of strangers. You would be taken into this small, scary, cave-like place where there was this strange man dressed from head to toe in a bizarre disguise that included a false beard and wellington boots. You were then either placed on his knee or made to stand next to him while he cuddled you and promised to bring you lots of new toys in the middle of the night. And parents were actually embarrassed when their young child kicked and screamed their way out of the place!

Britain was still a nation of shopkeepers and the streets were full of busy independent food, clothing and other specialist shops. There were no shopping malls, supermarkets or self-service shops until the late sixties and, even then, those that did exist were very small and rather dull places to shop; they were unsophisticated and not at all like the stylish shopping centres we have today. This was a time long before the days when future successive governments would encourage big-name retailers to dominate retailing, and local councils would stand by and allow the gradual demise of local high street shopping, turning once thriving town centres into pedestrianised ghost towns. It was in the days when the main roads were straddled with row upon row of small shops and your mum would drag you into each and every one of them when she took you shopping, and around every market stall as well. The downside was that when it was raining there was usually nowhere to shelter, so you just got wet.

At Christmas, high street shopping was so very different to today. You didn't see people walking around with silly red Santa Claus hats on and brightly coloured Bermuda shorts,

like you do now. No grown-up would ever have worn shorts out in the streets in wintertime, and men wouldn't even wear them in summertime unless they were in a holiday resort; definitely not in a large town or city. The new wave of 1960s clothing fashions were very popular with people of all ages and generally people took pride in their appearance when they were out and about. It was common practice to dress smartly to go high street shopping, especially if you were going to one of the main shopping areas in the city centre; that would be treated as a day out. Shopping for Christmas was a much more enjoyable experience than the boring routine of weekly food shopping, and so kids were much keener to go. The atmosphere was a lot more exciting and there were so many Christmassy things to see. The air in the street markets was filled with the smell of fresh pine Christmas trees and the market stalls were strung with hundreds of coloured festoon lights. There was always a man on the corner roasting chestnuts over red-hot coals in a brazier – another great smell of Christmas! Then there were the 'Del-Boy' illegal street traders selling cheap gonks and wind-up toys out of a suitcase. And, of course, the Salvation Army band would play festive music and sing carols on street corners. There were so many marvellous new space-age toys and games to see in the shops, and Woolworths always had the latest electric train set laid out on the counter with trains running around the track in both directions. But none of these toys, games and novelties seemed to impress your mum at all, nor did they distract her from the boring shopping list that she followed so rigidly. It seemed that there was nothing at all on the list for you. Food was always the main priority, and the only presents

being bought were unexciting things like socks, scarves, hankies and cigars for family and friends.

There were no use-by dates printed on food packaging in those days. In fact, there was much less packaging altogether and most food didn't come pre-packed in sealed plastic as it does today. Shops didn't open seven days a week from early 'til late, as they do now. Many still had half-day closing once a week, and were also shut on Saturday afternoons and all day on Sundays. Even the John Lewis flagship store in London's Oxford Street used to be shut on Saturday afternoons. Lots of shops would close at five o'clock in the evening. And many would shut for lunch! With these restricted shopping hours, mums needed to do a lot of strategic planning when buying food, drink and other perishables.

A traditional Christmas dinner was always considered to be roast turkey, but many people would have goose, chicken or capon for their Christmas roast dinner instead. But, whatever the choice, the bird had to be big enough to feed everyone that was coming for Christmas dinner, and provide leftovers for Boxing Day. It would be pre-ordered from the local butcher and picked up on Christmas Eve, along with all the other Christmas meats like ham and sausages. Most people bought their meat from a traditional local butchers' shop, fish from the local fishmonger, fruit and vegetables from the high street greengrocers and dairy products from the local dairy, or one of the shops supplied by the dairy. Milk, of course, was delivered – everyone had doorstep deliveries of milk each morning and the milk was in glass bottles. People would buy fresh bread from one of the many thousand bake-on-the-premises bakers' shops, which were often family businesses handed down from generation

to generation and commonly referred to as 'family bakers'. Such bakers could easily be identified from the other end of the street because it was traditional for them to have a large protruding green and gold 'Hovis' sign mounted on the wall above the shop, which acted like a homing beacon for anyone searching for them, not to mention the wonderfully enticing smell of freshly baked bread and cakes that could be smelt from some distance away.

Without the aid of sell-by dates on food packaging there was no way of telling how long something had been in the shop, let alone how long it had been in the food processing chain. But mums acquired the skill of detecting just how fresh things were by its appearance, texture and smell. By now, fridges were commonplace in average homes, but not domestic freezers, which didn't start to become widely owned until the 1970s. This meant that perishable foods could be kept in the fridge for a period of time, but without the benefit of a freezer the food stock had to be efficiently managed, especially over the Christmas period when all the shops would be closed until after Boxing Day. It wasn't unusual to see enormous queues gathering outside bakers' shops on the day before and the day after a holiday, especially Christmas. It was considered very important not to run out of bread; this was probably a tradition carried over from the 1940s or '50s, when a large doorstep slice of bread was often used to fend off hunger pangs between meals. In the 1960s a large cream bun was the more likely remedy. There were always back-up stocks of tinned foods to be bought, like Campbell's soup, corned beef, Fray Bentos meat pies and canned fruits in syrup. Oh, and the essential Carnation milk to pour over all those puddings and sweets. Not forgetting

a few cans of Kitekat for the cat, some Spiller's Winalot for the dog and a large box of Trill to keep the budgie bouncing with health over Christmas.

Woolworths was always the best place to buy affordable Christmas decorations and crackers, and market stalls would also have a good selection. The fairy lights were always a bit dodgy though, you had to be really careful in handling them when they were plugged into the mains, otherwise you could end up being the brightest light of them all. While mums were always in charge of Christmas shopping, your dad would be roped in to get the Christmas tree. In so many ways the 1960s was such a creative decade, but the artificial Christmas trees, which were so obviously fake, and the Christmas decorations, were all still quite primitive when compared to what is available today. It was always best to have a real Christmas tree, but they weren't as lush looking as most are nowadays. Back then they were mostly sad and sparse-looking silver firs that needed to be heavily dressed with tinsel, baubles and fairy lights to hide the tree's thinly covered branches, which would all too quickly shed their needles to form a lumpy green carpet on the floor below.

Christmas just wouldn't be Christmas if you didn't have a tipple of something special to offer guests, and even tee-total households would be sure to have at least a bottle of sherry and a bottle of port in the house during the Yuletide period. A tiny sip of these two sweet-tasting drinks are often remembered as being a child's first ever taste of anything alcoholic. The red and white wines that we now consume barrel loads of over Christmas were very expensive back then, and wine wasn't a popular choice of drink for ordinary people. In the 1960s, you might have found a bottle of

the then fashionable medium-sweet Mateus Rosé wine on the Christmas dinner table, but you were much more likely to have found a jug of water and several bottles of Double Diamond beer.

Christmas, 1965

The weather has been cold and wet throughout December, and although there has been much less rain in the last few days, it has got even colder. It's half-past seven on Christmas Eve morning and although you are fully awake, your whole body is still curled up underneath several layers of blankets and sheets, as warm as toast. You are in no hurry to investigate the new day, but you eventually poke your head out from beneath the bedcovers to test the temperature in the bedroom. Your worst suspicions are confirmed as your first warm breath hits the bedroom air and instantly forms a fog-like cloud; it is freezing out there! Having accustomed your face and nose to the chilly bedroom air, you decide to brave it and get up. The snazzy new bri-nylon carpet feels really cold under your bare feet and you can only find one slipper to put on. You must have kicked the other one under the bed when you got undressed last night. You switch on the transistor radio next to your bed and willingly expose your ears to the sound of The Who's latest record, *My Generation*, which you have turned to full volume, and is now bellowing out from Radio Caroline. While still trying to keep your one bare foot off the cold floor, you hop around the bed on your other slippered foot to take a peek out of the window and see what sort of day it is outside. It must have

been very cold overnight because ice has formed on the inside of the window and sadly, unlike last year, there is no picture-postcard Christmas snow scene to greet you as you pull back the curtains. After retrieving the lost slipper from under your bed, you hastily plug in the single-bar electric fire in the hope that it will quickly take some of the chill out of the air. Within a few minutes the ice on the window is starting to thaw and droplets of water are running down the pane, creating small pools on the sill below. The puddles of water soon grow bigger and begin to creep towards the edge. Realising that the water is about to overlap the sill and flow onto the edge of your bed, you rush downstairs to get a couple of used towels from the laundry basket to mop it up. You just about manage to get back to your room and throw the towels onto the windowsill in time to stop the water from cascading over your bed. This is a well-rehearsed ritual that you are well accustomed to performing on cold winter mornings, but you never manage to have anything close at hand to soak up the water. By now, the room has warmed up a bit and you realise that the fog-like breath you had been discharging into the bedroom air has disappeared.

Meanwhile, mum and dad are getting ready for work as usual. Although it's Christmas Eve, it's just another Friday and therefore a normal working day for grown-ups. Mum is hoping to finish work a bit early tonight so that she can get a few last-minute Christmas things for the big day tomorrow. By now it's about eight o'clock, and having visited the bathroom and got dressed, you sit on your bed for a moment or two listening to the end of the Rolling Stones' record, *Get Off My Cloud*, before turning off the radio and making your way downstairs. Even though mum has

The picture on the front of this 1961 *Jack and Jill* annual was apt for many parts of the UK that Christmas, with some areas getting enough snow for sledging.

had the kitchen stove turned on for ages, and the two-bar electric fire has been burning in the living room since dad got up an hour ago, the house still feels cold and draughty. It looks as though your day would be best spent indoors watching television, and perhaps one last search for hidden Christmas presents. Mind you, there is nothing much to interest you on television today until children's hour starts at five o'clock this afternoon with the *Five O'Clock Club*. They've got the Ivy League and Herman's Hermits on the show, so that should be good. There is a film on at two o'clock, *The Pickwick Papers*, which might be worth watching. But, other than that, it's just carol concerts and the dreaded *Crossroads*, complete with Amy Turtle and all that moving scenery. Tonight's television doesn't look too bad; there's *The Circus Comes to Town*, *Take Your Pick*, *Emergency Ward 10* and then *Ready Steady Go* with Cathy McGowan. It looks as though RSG is going to be another really good show, with tonight's guests including the Animals, the Kinks, The Who, the Hollies, Chris Farlowe and Herman's Hermits. That means Herman's Hermits are on television twice tonight – that's great!

The evening is filled with anticipation of tomorrow's big day. It has been a couple of weeks since you wrote and posted your letter to Father Christmas in Lapland telling him what presents you would like for Christmas, and explaining how good you have been, begging him not to forget you. There is not much more that you can do, other than leave the usual glass of sherry and a mince pie in the fireplace for when he comes down the chimney tonight. Oh, and you mustn't forget to leave a carrot out for Santa's reindeer, Rudolf. That is all you can do in the way of bribery; now you just have to

hope that Father Christmas can fit everything into his sack and that he can squeeze it all down the chimney. But it still bothers you as to how he is going to get down the chimney, what with the new electric fire mounted on the recently boarded-up fireplace. Mum and dad still haven't been able to convincingly explain that to you.

By now it's half-past eight and you are sitting on the floor in front of the television watching Cathy McGowan interviewing Roger Daltrey on *Ready Steady Go!* You are looking forward to seeing the Hollies sing their new record, *If I Needed Someone*. It's not one of their best records, but you just like the Hollies' music. Mum is in the kitchen sorting out a few things for tomorrow, and on the table behind you there is an annoying rustling of paper with last-minute wrapping of Christmas presents. There is a ring on the doorbell and everyone instinctively knows that it's just another group of carol singers collecting money. Everyone considers themselves to be too busy to answer the door and so the doorbell goes unanswered. Hopefully that will be the last of the door-to-door carol singers for this year. The last lot of carol singers that you answered the door to sounded like the cat's choir, and they only sang two lines of *Hark the Herald Angels Sing* before thrusting their hands out for money.

Everyone is so busy that your usual bedtime goes by completely unnoticed and you manage to watch the whole of *Peyton Place*, right through to half-past ten, before your mum eventually suggests that it's time you went to bed. Pleading with her that it's Christmas Eve doesn't carry much weight and so you finally give in and shuffle off on your wibbly-wobbly way to bed. Anyway, all the good television programmes have already finished and there is only

the news and religious programmes left to watch. Your mum will be in the kitchen until well after midnight and so your dad stays up and watches midnight mass, which is being televised this year from Waltham Abbey in Essex. When he does eventually turn off the television, he will probably fall asleep in his chair waiting for the little white dot to disappear from the screen.

Next morning arrives, and it is Christmas Day at last! It's only ten o'clock but you are up and dressed, and you have emptied the Christmas stocking that was on the end of your bed, done the family breakfast bit and opened your presents; all except for the one from granny, which you will open later when she arrives for Christmas dinner. Some pretty good presents this year, including a really flash, remote-controlled James Bond Aston Martin DB5 car. It's in a beautiful silver colour and it's got loads of fancy James Bond spy stuff on it, just like in the films. There's a bullet-proof shield that you can make go up and down, hidden machine guns that come out at the front and light up with machine-gun sounds, a push button ejector seat that throws the enemy through the sunroof and both licence plates revolve. But you can't try it out because you can't find the batteries to run it, so you are waiting for your dad to sort it out for you. You also got a Dalek shooting game, a Booma Boomerang, a *Stingray* television story book, a couple of stuffed Gonks and some Lego. Oh, and not forgetting the ten-bob note that auntie sent you in the post. You are pleased to see that your dad got the new Beatles' *Rubber Soul* LP for Christmas, but you are a little disappointed because it's the mono version, and you would have preferred the stereo version for when mum and dad get rid of the old mono record player

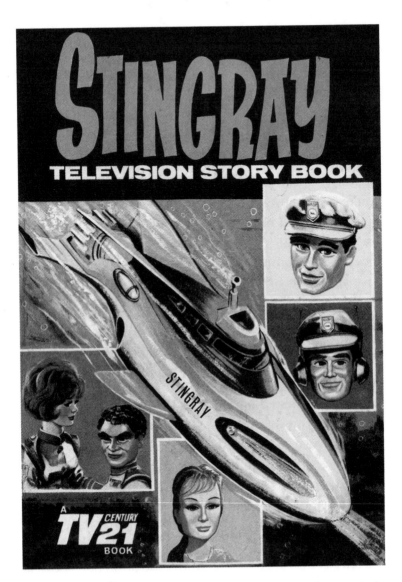

The *Stingray* children's marionette television series was created by Gerry and Sylvia Anderson and produced by AP films for Associated Television from 1964–65, with thirty-five half-hour episodes in all.

and buy a new stereo player with separate speakers. Never mind though, it still sounds great, just as long as it's played very loudly! Oh, and mum got a lovely new Tick-a-Tick-a-Timex watch.

You have lots of new toys and games to play with, but you find yourself curled up on the sofa in front of the television, folding a square sheet of paper into a multitude of sections to make your own fortune-teller finger game. And you're not even watching the latest episodes of *Supercar*, *Fireball XL5* and *Stingray* that are on ITV, but instead you are watching the 30-year-old Laurel and Hardy films that they're showing on BBC1. The antics of Laurel and Hardy have you in fits of laughter, so much so that your sides are beginning to ache, and you are enjoying it far too much to turn over for the *Adventure Showcase* on the other channel. Perhaps one day somebody will invent a television recording machine so that you don't have to miss anything on television ever again!

Everyone dressed up smart on Christmas Day, and there were lots of new brightly patterned Christmas jumpers proudly worn in every household especially for the day (whatever happened to them all after Christmas?). The table was laid early for Christmas dinner, with all the best glasses and cutlery, table napkins and Christmas crackers. And the dinner was always served sharp at one o'clock. It somehow seemed important to have it finished in time for the Queen's Christmas Message, which was always broadcast at three o'clock. Turkey was quite expensive and so many families had roast chicken or goose for their Christmas dinner, and plates were piled high with roast potatoes, stuffing, loads of vegetables and lashings of gravy. When you were

stuffed full of Christmas dinner, your mum would bring in the Christmas pudding, into which she had already put some sixpences or threepenny bits. It was considered to be lucky if you found one in your piece of pudding – extra lucky if you broke a tooth on one! As was the tradition, your dad would pour some of his Christmas brandy over the pudding and set fire to it. You would then struggle to eat the smallest piece of what was a very rich plum pudding, whilst trying to avoid swallowing one of the coins that were buried somewhere inside. In between dinner and teatime, you would munch on a variety of snacks laid out on the sideboard, from chestnuts and Twiglets to marshmallows and chocolates. It was the only day in the year that you could really stuff yourself silly. Sometime during the afternoon you would be prised away from the television to go outside for a walk out in the fresh air, to 'help your dinner go down'. Fortunately, you are back in time to watch *Disney Time* and play on the floor for a while with your new remote-controlled James Bond car before it's teatime and *Doctor Who* comes on the television at half-past six. Flicking through the *TV Times*, you are disappointed to see that ITV is showing *Thunderbirds* at the same time that *Doctor Who* is on BBC1. Why do they do that?

By late afternoon, you have succeeded in sampling every single snack on the sideboard, from Turkish delight to dried dates, and just when you feel that you have had enough, your mum starts to serve afternoon tea: cold turkey and ham sandwiches, sausage rolls and pickled onions, with lots of sweet things like mince pies, Victoria sponge cake, fruit jelly and blancmange. After tea, mum hands around her box of Black Magic chocolates that your dad bought her for

The *TV Times Extra* magazine from 1962.

Christmas, while dad puffs away on one of the half corona cigars that he was gifted. At last, granny prompts you to open the 'special' present she bought for you. It turns out to be a really great present, not the usual pair of socks or a set of hankies, but instead it's a fabulous Parker 51 fountain pen. It's the absolute bee's knees of fountain pens, more prized than the newer Parker 61 version. All of your friends at school will be really jealous!

Evening soon arrives and everyone is now full to the brim with Christmas food. Someone suggests playing a board game, but that's just too energetic a task for anyone to undertake and nobody has any brainpower left, so everyone sinks down into a cosy chair to watch the best of the evening's television programmes. Meanwhile, dad studies the Christmas *Radio Times* and *TV Times* magazines to see what's on. He is now firmly in charge of television viewing for the night, so will he let you watch *The Arthur Haynes Show* at half-past eight, or will he want to watch the Bing Crosby and Bob Hope film on the other side, *Road to Bali*? Yes, you end up watching the comedy film. However, there is good news because when the film ends the television is left on BBC1 for *The Ken Dodd Show* and your dad forgets all about *The Bruce Forsyth Show* on the other side, which he had been saying all day that he wanted to watch. Great!

It's now half-past ten, *The Ken Dodd Show* has just finished and everyone is chatting away, having lost interest in what's on television. It means that you can sit on the floor and watch the specially extended Christmas edition of *Top of the Pops*. And The Beatles are still number one with *Day Tripper*.

By the time television closes down for the night, you are fast asleep on the floor, and your mum has to wake you to

go to bed. Even on Christmas night all three of the television channels would close down at midnight, after which the grown-ups would usually play a board game or a game of cards for a while. But for kids that had managed to stay up late, it was now time for bed.

Ten

Memorable 1960s Events

First Man in Space

Wednesday 12 April 1961, Yuri Gagarin, the Soviet cosmonaut aboard *Vostok 1* spacecraft, became the first human in outer space and the first to orbit the Earth. After the flight, although Gagarin remained in the Soviet Air Force, he became a Soviet hero and somewhat of a celebrity, travelling the world to promote the Soviet achievement. He died on 27 March 1968 when his MiG-15 crashed while on a routine training flight. He was buried in the Kremlin Wall on Red Square in Moscow. He was 34.

Birth Control Pill

Monday 4 December 1961, the contraceptive pill was officially introduced into Britain when Enoch Powell, the

Conservative government's Minister of Health, announced that the oral contraceptive pill could in future be prescribed through the National Health Service at a subsidised price of 2s per month.

Satellite Television

Monday 23 July 1962, the first ever publicly available transatlantic satellite television signal was relayed by the Telstar 1 communications satellite. The first pictures were of the Statue of Liberty in New York and the Eiffel Tower, and the first broadcast included BBC's Richard Dimbleby in Brussels. That same evening, Telstar 1 relayed the first telephone call to be transmitted through space, and it successfully transmitted faxes, data and both live and taped television, including the first live transmission of television across an ocean, to Pleumeur-Bodou in north-west France.

Cuban Missile Crisis

October 1962 is generally regarded as the time when the Cold War, primarily between the USA and the USSR, came closest to becoming a nuclear war, when United States intelligence discovered that the Cuban and Soviet governments had placed nuclear missiles in Cuba during the preceding weeks and that they were building missile bases. During the crisis, the US government sought to do all it could to ensure removal of the missiles. The crisis ended on 28 October 1962, when President John F. Kennedy and the United Nations Secretary-General U. Thant reached agreement with Soviet premier Nikita Khrushchev for the dismantling and return of weapons

to the Soviet Union. This was in exchange for President Kennedy's undertaking to remove all US missiles from Turkey and an arrangement with regard to future respect of Cuban borders and its sovereignty.

Beatlemania

The media first used the term 'Beatlemania' in early 1963, soon after The Beatles had achieved their first UK number one hit single, *Please Please Me*. Beatlemania was the name used to describe the intense levels of hysteria shown by fans whenever The Beatles were seen in public anywhere in the UK. Early in 1964 the phenomenon spread to America, when The Beatles made their first visit there following the success of their single, *I Want to Hold Your Hand*, which was their first number one hit single in the US Billboard Hot 100 chart. Beatlemania was at its height from 1963–65, when The Beatles were touring extensively and made the films *Hard Day's Night* (1964) and *Help!* (1965).

Great Train Robbery

This was the name given to the £2.6 million robbery from a Glasgow–Euston night train that took place when the train reached Bridego Railway Bridge, Ledburn, near Mentmore in Buckinghamshire on Monday 8 August 1963. The robbery was carried out by a London gang, which numbered about fifteen in total. Thirteen of the gang were soon caught and in April 1964 the seven main culprits were each sentenced to thirty years imprisonment. These included Ronnie Biggs, who managed to escape from prison after serving only fifteen months. He fled first to Paris, then Australia and then to Brazil, where he remained until 2001

when he voluntarily returned to the UK. He was arrested on his arrival in the UK and re-imprisoned to serve the remainder of his thirty-year sentence. Biggs suffered a lot of ill health while in prison and on 6 August 2009, the day before his 80th birthday, he was released from custody on 'compassionate grounds'.

Assassination of John F. Kennedy

John F. Kennedy, 35th President of the United States, was assassinated in Dallas, Texas, on Friday 22 November 1963, at the age of 46. Lee Harvey Oswald was arrested and charged with the assassination. Oswald denied the charge and was killed by Jack Ruby on Sunday 24 November before he could be indicted or tried.

BBC2 Launch

The third British television channel, BBC2, was launched during the evening of Monday 20 April 1964, but due to a huge power failure only brief news bulletins could be shown that evening. The first programme to be officially shown on the new channel was *Play School*, which was broadcast the following morning, Tuesday 21 April 1964.

BIBA Opens in London

Monday 7 September 1964, Barbara Hulanicki, fashion designer, and her husband Stephen Fitz-Simon, opened the first BIBA ladies fashion boutique in what was previously a small chemist's shop at 87 Abingdon Road, Kensington, London. BIBA quickly became an important and famous part of the sixties fashion revolution.

From September 16th
Choose your post

Of course all letters are important. But some are more urgent than others.

So now you're going to have a choice.

The New Letter Service with two speeds. And we're going to call it "First Class" and "Second Class" post.

First Class at 5d.

Second Class at 4d.

A *fivepenny* stamp will normally get your letter to anywhere in the U.K. the next day.

A *fourpenny* letter will take about a day longer.

You put on the right stamp—we do the rest.

Whether you spend 4d or 5d, two-speed service will be dependable.

September 16th.

That's the starting date.

Also from that date you can seal the envelopes of all letters, both

first and second class. This makes things safer for the contents, and easier for our sorting machines.

So you see the New Letter Service isn't only two-speed and two-price.

It's also two-way.

You benefit.

We benefit.

yours faithfully   The Post Office

The Post Office introduced the two-class postal system on 16 September 1968.

Winston Churchill's Funeral

Saturday 30 January 1965, a televised state funeral was held at St Paul's Cathedral in London after Churchill's body had lain in state for three days. The funeral was attended by many of the world's leaders.

First Moon Orbit

Sunday 3 April 1966, *Luna 10*, the Soviet spacecraft, became the first unmanned space probe to enter orbit around the moon.

England Win the FIFA World Cup

Saturday 30 July 1966, England beat West Germany 4–2 after extra time at London's old Wembley Stadium in front of a 98,000-strong crowd, to win the final of the 1966 FIFA

World Cup and the Jules Rimet Trophy, thereby becoming the first host nation to win the tournament since Italy in 1934. Managed by Alf Ramsey (knighted in 1967), the England team for the final was Gordon Banks, George Cohen, Jack Charlton, Bobby Moore (c), Ray Wilson, Nobby Stiles, Alan Ball, Bobby Charlton, Martin Peters, Geoff Hurst and Roger Hunt. The England goal scorers were Hurst (3) 18', 98', 120' and Peters (1) 78'. The German goal scorers were Haller (1) 12' and Weber (1) 90'. The other eleven members of the England squad who helped get England to the final were Jimmy Armfield, Peter Bonette, Gerry Byrne, Ian Callaghan, John Connelly, George Eastham, Ron Flowers, Jimmy Greaves, Norman Hunter, Terry Paine and Ron Springett.

Sgt Pepper's Lonely Hearts Club Band

Thursday 1 June 1967, The Beatles released their famous *Sgt Pepper's Lonely Hearts Club Band* album.

Bank's First ATMs

Tuesday 27 June 1967, the world's first electronic ATM (automated teller machine) was installed at a branch of Barclays Bank in Enfield, north London. Reg Varney, star of the *On the Buses* television comedy series, fronted the advertising campaign for the new machine. (In 1939 there had been a one-off tryout of an ATM by the City Bank of New York, but that ATM was removed after six months due to lack of customer acceptance.)

Heart Transplant

Sunday 3 December 1967, the first human-to-human heart transplant operation was performed by South African cardiac surgeon, Dr Christiaan Barnard.

Assassination of Martin Luther King Jr

Thursday 4 April 1968, the American Civil Rights leader, Martin Luther King Jr, was assassinated in Memphis Tennessee, USA, at the age of 39.

Assassination of Robert F. Kennedy

Wednesday 5 June 1968, the United States Senator, Robert F. Kennedy, was assassinated in a crowded kitchen passageway as he made his way out of the Ambassador Hotel in Los Angeles, California. He was 42.

First Manned Orbit of the Moon

Tuesday 24 December 1968, *Apollo 8*, the American space mission, with astronauts Lovell, Anders and Borman, became the first manned space mission to orbit the moon.

Concorde's First Flight

Sunday 2 March 1969, the turbojet-powered supersonic passenger airliner, Concorde, made its first flight. However, it didn't begin passenger service until 21 January 1976 (retired from service on 26 November 2003).

London's Victoria Line Opens

Friday 7 March 1969, the Queen officially opened the London Underground's Victoria Line at a ceremony that took place at Victoria Station in London.

It was on 21 July 1969 that man first walked on the moon.

First Man on the Moon

Sunday 20 July 1969, *Apollo 11*, the American space mission, with astronauts Armstrong, Collins and Aldrin, became the first manned space mission to land on the moon, and Armstrong and Aldrin became the first humans to set foot on its surface – Wednesday 16 July 1969 (launch), Sunday 20 July 1969 (*Eagle* landed), Monday 21 July 1969 (moonwalk).

Woodstock Festival

The world-famous three-day peace and music event was held at Max Yasgur's 600-acre dairy farm near the rural village of White Lake, Bethel, Sullivan County, New York, over the weekend of 15–18 August 1969.

Vietnam War

This military conflict took place in Vietnam, Laos and Cambodia throughout the 1960s (1959 to 30 April 1975). The war was fought between the communists of North Vietnam, supported by its communist allies, and the government of South Vietnam, supported by the United States and some other member nations of the South-East Asia Treaty Organisation (SEATO). Britain didn't enter into the Vietnam War, but the war got a lot of news coverage here, and there were several anti-war demonstrations held in London from 1963–68.

Eleven

WHATEVER HAPPENED TO?

Adam Faith. He had twenty-three hit singles from November 1959 to June 1965, including eleven top-ten hits, of which two reached number one, *What Do You Want* in November 1959, and *Poor Me* in January 1960. In the late 1960s he turned to music management and acting, getting the starring role in the 1970s television series, *Budgie*, and roles in several films, including *Stardust*, *McVicar* and *Foxes*. He continued to do work for television and in 1992 got the starring role in the television series, *Love Hurts*. In the 1980s he got involved in the world of finance and became a financial investment adviser and financial journalist whist continuing with his acting work. He suffered with heart problems and, in 1986, underwent surgery. In 2001, his financial investments failed and he was declared bank-

rupt. He became ill after his stage performance in *Love and Marriage* at Stoke-on-Trent and died of a heart attack early the following morning on Saturday 8 March 2003, aged 62.

Alan 'Fluff' Freeman. He started his British career as a disc jockey on Radio Luxembourg in the late 1950s, but achieved nationwide fame when he joined the BBC Light Programme in 1961 and began presenting *Pick of the Pops*, which he continued to present after Radio 1 replaced the old BBC Light Programme in 1967. He presented *Pick of the Pops* off and on until 1972, and then stayed with Radio 1 until 1979, when he went to work for London's Capital Radio until 1988, returning to BBC Radio 1 for the period 1989–93. He then did work for several other radio stations before returning again to the BBC to work on BBC Radio 2 from 1997–2000, by which time he was 73. In 1998 he was appointed an MBE, and in 2000 he was presented with a Lifetime Achievement Award at the Sony Radio Awards in London. In later life he suffered badly from arthritis and was forced to use a walking frame. He died on 27 November 2006 after a short illness at Brinsworth House, Twickenham – a retirement home for members of the acting and entertainment professions. He was 79. His many memorable catchphrases included 'Hi there, pop pickers!', 'Greetings, music lovers!', 'Alright? Stay bright!' and 'Not Arf!'.

Billy Fury. He had twenty-three hit singles in the early to mid-sixties, including ten top-ten hits, but he suffered from heart problems and was forced to become much less active. Despite ongoing trouble with his heart, he continued to work through until his death in 1983. Sadly, on 27 January that year he collapsed after returning home from the recording studio, and died the next morning at the age of 42.

Cathy McGowan. She came to fame in 1964 when, as a 19-year-old from Streatham working as a £10 a week junior in the fashion department of *Woman's Own*, she beat hundreds of other 'typical teenage' girl applicants to become an adviser on one of the top British pop music and 'cult-mod' television shows of the 1960s, *Ready Steady Go!* She was soon installed as the show's co-presenter, eventually presenting it on her own. Her fashion sense, street-wise knowledge and girl-next-door presentation style proved to be popular with teenage mods who were big followers of the show, which regularly featured many of their favourite groups and artists, including the Small Faces, the Spencer Davis

Cathy McGowan on the cover of *TV Times* in March 1965, and Vanessa Redgrave with Simon Dee on the cover of *The Simon Dee Book* in 1968.

Group, the Rolling Stones, The Who, Dusty Springfield, Dionne Warwick and Marvin Gaye. Mods regarded Cathy as one of them and she soon became known as 'Queen of the Mods'. She continued to present *RSG* until it ended on 23 December 1966. During the sixties, Cathy also worked in journalism, did modelling and presented a show on Radio Luxembourg. In 1970 she married actor Hywel Bennett, but the marriage was dissolved in 1988. She joined the board of London's Capital Radio when it started up in 1973. In the late eighties she worked as an entertainment journalist for the BBC's Newsroom South-East, interviewing celebrities, including the singer/actor Michael Ball who was to become her long-term partner. She has continued to do journalistic and broadcasting work, but mainly helps with the career of her partner and does charity work. Cathy, an icon of the 1960s, is now a grandmother in her 60s, but still looks fabulous and remains 'Queen of the Mods'.

Charlie Drake. One of Britain's best loved comedians, known for his catchphrase 'Hallo, my darlings!' He made his name in the 1950s as a comedy actor, singer and writer on stage and in film and television. His slapstick style of comedy continued to be popular throughout the 1960s and, apart from a two year enforced break early in the decade, as a result of serious injuries he suffered while performing a slapstick sketch and a later car accident, he remained on our television screens throughout the rest of the sixties in shows like *The Charlie Drake Show*, *The Worker* and *Who is Sylvia?* He also co-wrote and starred in four sixties films: *Sands of the Desert* (1960), *Petticoat Pirates* (1961), *The Cracksman* (1963) and *Mister Ten Per Cent* (1967). He released eleven records during the 1960s, but only

two made it into the UK top twenty, *Mr Custer* reaching number twelve in 1960 and *My Boomerang Won't Come Back* reaching number fourteen in 1961. He continued to be successful in television comedy throughout the 1970s, but in the 1980s he turned to straight acting, appearing in such plays as Shakespeare's *As You Like It*, Harold Pinter's *The Caretaker* and BBC's adaptation of Dickens' *Bleak House*. In the 1990s, he appeared with Jim Davidson in the adult pantomime *SINderella*. In 1995 he retired after suffering a stroke and then stayed at Brinsworth House, Twickenham – a retirement home especially for members of the acting and entertainment professions. He died on 23 December 2006 following a long illness. He was 81.

Donovan. A singer-songwriter and guitarist icon of the mid-to-late 1960s, Donovan was first discovered by ITV's pop music television show, *Ready Steady Go!* He came to fame following a series of live performances on the show and soon became internationally famous for his folk/pop style of music, and was recognised for dressing halfway between the beatnik and hippie styles of fashion. Donovan was one of the leading British recording artists of the late sixties, with eleven hit singles from 1965–69, including seven UK top-ten hits. His biggest hit record was *Sunshine Superman*, which reached number two in the UK and topped the charts in the USA. He also had several hit albums both in the UK and in the USA. Donovan's hits dried up after he split with record producer Mickey Most in late 1969, after which he left the music industry for a while. His style of music fell from favour in the 1970s and '80s, and he only performed and recorded occasionally during that period. Greatest hits and tribute albums

continued to be released throughout that time and in the 1990s and 2000s. He released a new album, Beat Café, in 2004. In 2005 his autobiography *The Hurdy Gurdy Man* was published. In 2007 he released his first ever DVD, *The Donovan Concert Live in LA*. In the 2000s Donovan has continued to tour and perform live concerts in the UK and USA, and he is currently working on a new album, which is said to have the working title, *Ritual Groove*.

Harold Wilson. British Labour party politician who became leader of the Labour Party following the death of Hugh Gaitskell in 1963. He won the general election in 1964 and was Prime Minister from 1964–70. He regarded himself as a 'man of the people' and usually looked the part, often seen smoking a pipe and wearing a Gannex raincoat. His time as Prime Minister was problematical, with his imposition of strict wage controls and prices, raised taxes, the devaluation of the pound in 1967, the failed reform of the House of Lords and unsuccessful attempt to enter the European Community (EC). In 1966 Wilson got a mention in The Beatles' song *Taxman*, from the Revolver album, with the lyrics 'Don't ask me what I want it for (Taxman Mister Wilson)'. In June 1970 he was defeated in the general election by the Conservative Party, led by Edward Heath. Wilson continued as leader of the Labour Party in opposition and in 1974 he became Prime Minister for the second time. However, on 16 March 1976, at the age of 60, he announced his resignation as Prime Minister and was succeeded by James Callaghan. Later that same year he was awarded a knighthood. Wilson remained MP for Huyton until he retired from the House of Commons in 1983, when he was made Baron Wilson of Rievaulx, after Rievaulx

Abbey in his native Yorkshire. Following his retirement, he suffered with Alzheimer's disease and soon withdrew from public life. He died of colon cancer in May 1995 at the age of 79. His memorial service was held at Westminster Abbey on 13 July 1995 and he was buried in a simple ceremony at the nineteenth-century church of St Mary the Virgin, St Mary's, the largest of his beloved Scilly Islands, off England's south-west coast, where he had regularly holidayed.

Helen Shapiro. Given the nickname 'Foghorn' by her school friends because of her deep tone voice, Helen was just 14 years old when she first topped the UK charts with *Walking Back to Happiness* and she is still the youngest female artist to have reached number one in the UK charts. When her first record was released early in 1961 she was unable to play it at home because her family didn't have a record player, and she had to go round to a neighbour's to listen to it. Helen had ten top-forty hits in the early 1960s, including two number ones, *You Don't Know* (1961) and *Walking Back to Happiness* (1961), and three others that made it into the top ten: *Don't Treat Me Like a Child* (1961), *Tell Me What He Said* (1962) and *Little Miss Lonely* (1962). Most of her recording sessions were at the famous EMI Abbey Road studios in London (before The Beatles). In October 1961 she topped the bill on ATV's *Sunday Night at the London Palladium*, and was still back at her school desk on the Monday morning. The Beatles were among the list of supporting acts on her national tour of 1963. In 1964 Helen's popularity began to wane as newer female singers like Dusty Springfield, Cilla Black, Sandie Shaw and Lulu became popular, and she was seen as being old fashioned and not part of the new 'swinging sixties' music scene. By then she had already started to

Helen Shapiro, the early 1960s schoolgirl chart-topper, seen here on the front page of the *New Musical Express* in June 1961. She later had The Beatles as one of her supporting acts on her national Helen Shapiro Tour of 1963.

branch out doing the jazz music she had always loved. She later moved into acting, both on stage and on television, and in the 1980s played Nancy for a year in the West End production of *Oliver!* She joined up with Humphrey Lyttelton in the 1980s and they toured together for seventeen years in a series of 'Hump and Helen' jazz concerts. During that period she also toured with her own show, *Simply Helen*. In 1993 her autobiography was published, and in 1995 she was the subject of television's *This is Your Life*. Helen became a believer in Jesus in 1987. In 2002, after a total of forty-two years of touring, she retired from showbusiness to concentrate on her Gospel Outreach work, which she is scheduled to continue with in 2010.

Monica Rose (*Double Your Money*). The petite 'chirpy cockney' and former accounts clerk from White City in London came to fame in 1964 when, as a 16-year-old, she appeared as a contestant on ITV's *Double Your Money* quiz show and proved to be so popular with the audience and the show's host, Hughie Green, that she was invited to become a regular hostess. She stayed with the show for three years, returning for a short time in 1968 before the show was finally axed. In 1970 she was reunited with Hughie Green when they co-hosted a new ITV television game show, *The Sky's the Limit*. She then went into cabaret where she performed a singing and comedy act, and she also appeared in pantomime. In 1977 she left showbusiness and three years later was admitted to hospital, suffering from depression and nervous exhaustion. In 1982 she married Terry Dunnell, a Baptist lay-preacher. She subsequently became a Christian and took a job as a checkout operator in a supermarket near her home in Leicester. However, she continued to suffer

with ill-health and on 4 February 1994 she died in her sleep at home. She was 45.

Muriel Young. Appointed by Associated-Rediffusion as the first continuity announcer for the new ITV commercial television channel when it started up in 1955, Muriel Young became one of the most recognised faces on television in the 1960s. The former model and actress did a broad range of television presenting and interviewing work, but she is best known for the six years she spent presenting ITV's children's television shows alongside Wally Whyton and Bert Weedon. Known affectionately as 'Auntie Mu' to her young fans, she presented shows including *Small Time* (1959–66) with glove puppet Pussy Cat Willum, *Tuesday Rendezvous* (1961–63) with glove puppets Ollie Beak and Fred Barker, *Five O'Clock Club* (1963–65) and *Ollie and Fred's Five O'Clock Club* (1965–66). She also worked as a disc jockey on Radio Luxembourg in the early sixties. Late in the decade she set up a children's department for Granada Television, and in the 1970s she produced a series of successful pop programmes for younger viewers. In 1972 she devised and produced Granada Television's long-running film magazine programme for children, *Clapperboard*, hosted by Chris Kelly. She was also a regular judge on the 1970–80s television talent show, *New Faces*. In 1983–84 she produced and presented two series of *Ladybirds*, a Channel 4 programme made by Mike Mansfield's independent company, in which she interviewed popular female singers of the day. Muriel retired in 1986 after more than thirty years in television, and moved with her husband, Cyril Coke, back to County Durham where she was born. In retirement, she spent more time on her hobby of oil painting,

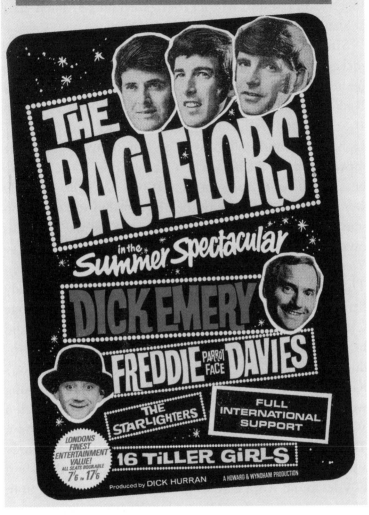

A poster advertising The Bachelors' Summer Spectacular at the Victoria Palace Theatre in London, *c.* 1969.

and exhibited her work, mainly landscapes, locally and at Liberty's in London. Muriel Young died on 24 March 2001 at Stanhope, County Durham. She was 72.

Simon Dee. The previously little known actor and disc jockey's earliest claim to fame was being the first voice to be heard on the now famous offshore pirate radio station, Radio Caroline, when it started broadcasting on 29 March 1964. In 1965 he left Radio Caroline to join the BBC Light Programme and to work on Radio Luxembourg. He moved to BBC Radio 1 when it opened in 1967, and also became one of the presenters of BBC's *Top of the Pops*. He went on to become one of the biggest radio and television stars of the 1960s when, in the same year, he was given his own early evening live chat show on BBC television, *Dee Time*. He also hosted the Miss World contest at the Lyceum Theatre in London, in November 1967. He was already flamboyant in the way he behaved and dressed, but the huge television viewing figures for his show went to his head and he began to act the part of a superstar, quarrelling with production staff and bosses, and cruising up and down London's Kings Road in his Aston Martin DB5 with beautiful young women companions. In 1970 he switched to ITV's London Weekend Television to host the late-night Sunday show, *The Simon Dee Show*, but the show was dropped after only a few months. Having fallen out with both the BBC and ITV, he found work hard to get and soon disappeared from the airwaves altogether. His sudden fall from grace was one of the fastest in broadcasting history. By late 1970 he was signing on the dole at the Fulham Road Labour Exchange. He then took a job as a trainee bus driver, but that didn't last long. In 1974, he served a brief term in prison for non-

payment of rates on his former Chelsea home. Later in the 1970s he made brief comebacks as a DJ on local radio. By the early 1980s he was being described in the newspapers as a recluse. In 1988 he briefly hosted *Sounds of the Sixties* on BBC Radio 2, but it didn't last and further sporadic attempts at a comeback to TV or radio failed. Simon Dee died of bone cancer at the Royal Hampshire County Hospital, Winchester on 30 August 2009. He was 74.

Valerie Singleton. Best known as the 1960s co-presenter of BBC's *Blue Peter*, having, in September 1962, taken over from Anita West who had bridged the gap as stand-in host after Leila Williams left the show in January that year. Valerie presented the first *Blue Peter* charity appeal (1962), introduced *Blue Peter*'s first pet, a brown and white mongrel dog named Petra (1962), wore the first *Blue Peter* badge (1963), appeared in the first *Blue Peter* book (1964) and took part in the first filming trip abroad (Norway in 1965). In 1972 she stopped being a main presenter of *Blue Peter* (replaced by Leslie Judd), but continued to appear regularly as a roving reporter. From 1972–81 she presented a spin-off series, *Blue Peter Special Assignment*, which was initially filmed in various European cities, but later ventured much further afield to such places as Singapore and Canada. She also presented *Val Meets … The VIPs* for BBC1 television from 1973–74, with famous guests including Morecambe and Wise, and Margaret Thatcher (then Secretary of State for Education and Science in Prime Minister Edward Heath's Conservative government). From 1974–78 she also worked for the BBC news and current affairs television series, *Nationwide*, as a 'consumer unit' presenter. In 1978 she presented the BBC's late-night news programme, *Tonight*,

replacing Sue Lawley. In the 1980s and '90s, she presented several radio and television programmes, including BBC2's *The Money Programme*, and Radio 4's *PM* programme. Having also presented a travel programme for ITV, she is now a travel writer for several publications. In 2005, at the age of 68, she moved from her long-time home in London to live in Dorset. She still appears regularly in all forms of the media, including occasional guest appearances on *Blue Peter*.